Recruiting Black and Minority Ethnic Adopters and Foster Carers

Gwen Rule

BAAF
ADOPTION
& FOSTERING

Supported by
LONDON
COUNCILS

Supported by

FCA®
Foster Care Associates

Published by
**British Association for Adoption & Fostering
(BAAF)**
Saffron House
6–10 Kirby Street
London EC1N 8TS
www.baaf.org.uk

Charity Registration 275689

© BAAF 2006

British Library Cataloguing in Publication Data
A catalogue record for this book is available from the
British Library

ISBN 1 903699 91 6

Project management by Shaila Shah, Director of
Publications, BAAF
Photograph on cover posed by models by John Birdsall
www.johnbirdsall.co.uk
Designed by Andrew Haig & Associates
Typeset by Aldgate Press, London
Printed in Great Britain by The Lavenham Press
Trade distribution by Turnaround Publisher Services,
Unit 3, Olympia Trading Estate, Coburg Road, London
N22 6TZ

BAAF is the leading UK-wide membership
organisation for all those concerned with adoption,
fostering and child care issues.

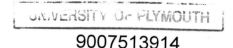

Contents

Acknowledgements

Thanks to Hedi Argent and Eileen Fursland for their valuable input and editorial guidance and to Jennifer Cousins, Alexandra Plumtree and Ravinder Kaur for their contributions. Also thanks to Katrina Wilson, Shaila Shah, Jeffrey Coleman, Savita DeSousa, Tana Thomas, Sally Baffour, Roana Roach and Jo Francis for the support that I received.

Thanks also to the numerous agencies which made a contribution to this guide, with particular thanks to NCH Black Families, a large local authority in South East England, London Borough of Tower Hamlets, Marion Hundleby at the North London Consortium, and Kirklees Metropolitan Borough Council, for their contributions. All case studies and quotations, if not attributed in the text, have been derived from feedback from members of the London Black Adopters Group, which was initiated by Gwen Rule and is co-facilitated by Gwen Rule and Roana Roach.

Gwen Rule
October 2006

Note about the author

Gwen Rule is the Development and Training Officer for the BAAF-ALG Black and Minority Ethnic Carer Recruitment Project, and is based in the BAAF Southern England Regional Team. In addition to her promotion of recruitment strategies that engage effectively with minority communities, last year Gwen also set up the innovative BAAF Black Adopters' Support Group.

Gwen has worked for BAAF since September 2002. She trained originally as a teacher, and before joining BAAF she worked in various spheres of education, including work with children having special needs, and in teacher recruitment.

BAAF is grateful for the support of Foster Care Associates.

This guide is part of a BAAF project to recruit black and minority ethnic adopters and foster carers, funded by London Councils (formerly the Association for Local Government (ALG)).

1 Introduction

Children from black, Asian and mixed-heritage backgrounds who are in the care system wait far longer than white children for a permanent family because there are not enough black, Asian and mixed ethnicity families available to adopt them. More families are urgently needed to give these children the best possible chance in life.

This Good Practice Guide aims to help anyone who may be involved in the recruitment of carers from black and minority ethnic communities. It looks at the factors that impact on recruitment and presents examples of approaches which agencies have found successful in reaching prospective adopters and foster carers in these communities.

In the following chapters, this guide:

- **Examines the context**: the need for permanence; the numbers of black and minority ethnic children in care; the effects of transracial adoption; issues of identity and racism; the shortfall of black and minority ethnic adoptive families; and an overview of efforts that have been made to recruit carers for black, Asian and mixed-heritage children.

- **Outlines the legal framework and guidance** issued to agencies on finding placements for these children.

- **Looks at policy and practice**, with examples of how adoption agencies go about the task of finding ethnically and culturally matched placements for black, Asian and mixed-heritage children.

- **Considers black and minority ethnic communities in Britain**: their main geographical locations and faiths and the social, economic and environmental factors that may be holding back black and Asian families from becoming carers.

- **Looks at recruitment policies and planning**, with examples from different agencies.

- **Suggests a wide range of effective ways of reaching carers** from black and minority ethnic communities and considers how best to prepare and support these carers.

- **Provides examples of good practice** in a number of different agencies and projects.

- **Provides further resources and references.**

Although this guide is mainly about recruiting black and Asian carers, agencies may find many of the ideas and suggestions useful when trying to recruit from any specific group or community, including white minority ethnic groups.

The children

It was not until 2001 that the Department of Health (England and Wales) began to collate statistical information on the ethnic profile of children looked after by local authorities, and since this information has become available, it has shown that there has been an increase in the number of black and mixed-heritage children coming into the care system.

The Department for Education and Skills (DfES) figures for looked after children as at 31 March 2005 revealed that, in England:

- eight per cent of looked after children were of mixed-heritage (an increase of 1% since 2001);

- a further eight per cent of children were black or black British (another increase of 1% since 2001);

- Asian children made up three per cent of the looked after population (an increase of 1% on the previous year);

- two per cent were listed as 'other ethnic groups';

- the figure for white children had decreased by two per cent since 2001.

In all, then, 21 per cent of the children looked after in England in 2005 were black, Asian or of mixed-heritage.

Yet only 7.9 per cent of the UK general population is from non-white ethnic groups, according to the 2001 Census (9% in England; 2% in both Scotland and Wales, and less than 1% in Northern Ireland).

So it is clear that black and minority ethnic children are over-represented in the care system and that more black, Asian and mixed-heritage families are needed to provide secure ethnically matched placements for these children.

Finding adults from these communities who have the practical and emotional resources to become foster carers or adoptive parents may be difficult for some agencies but it is not an impossible task.

Terminology

There is considerable debate about the terminology used to characterise groups of people based on their background, culture and heritage. No single term will meet everyone's requirements. In addition, ethnicity is self-defined and is often grounded in shared family values and beliefs that relate to culture, heritage, religion, nationality, language and, in some circumstances, even to personal appearance. This needs to be borne in mind when using statistical information that is collated according to skin colour, such as that from the Census.

The main focus of this guide is on recruiting carers for children who are black, Asian or of mixed-heritage.

- *Black* is used throughout this guide as a generic term in reference to children and adults who are non-white and whose roots originate from Africa or the Caribbean.

- *Asian* is used to refer to people from South Asian backgrounds: India, Pakistan and Bangladesh.

- *Mixed-heritage* refers to children and adults whose birth parents come from different ethnic groups.

- *Black and minority ethnic* is used as a general term to encompass both black and Asian people and those from, for example, China, Malaysia, Vietnam and various countries in the Middle East, as well as those of mixed-heritage.

Maintaining confidentiality

All the examples of policies and practice identified in the guide are attributable to specific agencies, but not all have been named.

Throughout the guide, comments from prospective adopters, approved adopters and foster carers are quoted in the text. Many of these comments were given as feedback to the author by email when she asked members of a black adopters' support group about their experiences of the adoption process. These comments are quoted anonymously in order to protect people's identities.

Other quotations are taken from collections of writing by people who have either adopted or been adopted, and these are attributed in the text.

2 The context

The need for permanence

The DfES consultation document on care planning and special guardianship (2004) says:

> Every child needs to feel secure within a loving family. They need connections with adults who are committed to them long term, who will always be there for them and who care about what happens to them. In practice this means supporting their development and their transition through childhood to adulthood. We call the framework of emotional, physical and legal conditions that gives a child a sense of security, continuity, commitment and identity – permanence.

The Department of Health (1998) circular, *Adoption: Achieving the right balance*, stated that the key objectives for the Government were to tackle poor outcomes and the lack of stability for looked after children. The circular also highlighted that, while significant progress had been made by agencies in relation to minority ethnic children, more work still needed to be done.

Although these documents were published for England and Wales, they highlight the clear need for permanence for all children in the UK.

It is fundamental to the White Paper on Adoption (Department of Health, 2000a) to ensure that all children are placed with carers who are capable of providing safe and effective care, throughout childhood and beyond. Studies by Falhberg (1994) and Thoburn (1994) have emphasised that two essential elements of well-being are hardest to provide for separated children:

- a sense of permanence and stability; and

- a sense of personal and cultural identity.

The shortage of placements

Of the 70,000 children looked after in the UK, around 8,000 are waiting for a permanent placement.

In England in 2005 there were 60,900 children being looked after – 79 per cent of these were white. As previously stated, 19 per cent were of black, Asian or mixed-heritage origin and two per cent were of "other" ethnicity. (National Statistics, 2006). Black and minority ethnic communities have settled in many of the main cities in England; however, the largest grouping of BME communities can be found in London. The Greater London Authority (GLA) (2004) reported that black and minority ethnic communities make up 28 per cent of the population in London.

In Scotland, there were over 12,000 children being looked after by local authorities but 57 per cent of these were being looked after at home by their parents or family or friends; 29 per cent were with foster carers or prospective adopters; and 13 per cent in residential accommodation. Numbers of children from minority ethnic communities were small. Apart from the "unknown" category where children's ethnic origin was unknown or unreported, the largest ethnic group was the mixed ethnicity group, with 95 children (National Statistics, 2006).

In Wales, excluding children looked after under an agreed series of short-term placements, there were 4,668 children being looked after. Of these, 73 per cent were in foster care placements. Again, numbers of children from minority ethnic groups were small. The largest group (after the "unknown" group) was of mixed ethnicity, numbering 114 children.

In Northern Ireland there were 2,531 looked after children as at 31 March 2005. Just over 56 per cent (1,432) were in foster care, with 26.6 per cent (674) placed with family, 12.5 per cent (317) in residential accommodation, and 4.3 per cent (108) in other types of accommodation. A full breakdown of ethnicity is not available in the official statistics. Between 1999 and 2005, it is estimated that 500 looked after children were adopted in Northern Ireland.

A study carried out for NCH (Selwyn *et al*, 2004) concluded that there is a shortage of *all* minority ethnic adopters and, in particular, a desperate need for black, black mixed-heritage and mixed relationship adopters.

There is a shortfall of foster placements too. In a survey carried out in September 2004, The Fostering Network (2004) estimated that there is a need for an additional 10,000 foster carers across the UK: 8,200 in England, 1,700 in Scotland, 750 in Wales and 350 in Northern Ireland. These are the numbers of foster carers who would have to be recruited in order to offer placement choice so that each child can live with a family who meets their individual needs.

A shortage of this magnitude contributes to instability and disruption in the lives of children and young people. It also implies that many children and young people are in foster placements which are not ethnically or culturally matched. Given that many foster carers offer long-term or permanent care and that some eventually become adopters, increasing the number of foster carers from black and minority ethnic communities is as important as increasing the number of adopters.

The Fostering Network surveyed 78 fostering services in 2005–6 for its report, *Improving Effectiveness in Foster Care Recruitment*. Half of the fostering services had a target to recruit carers from specific minority ethnic groups. The targets varied throughout the country, but a number of London boroughs reported shortages of white British foster carers and foster carers for unaccompanied asylum seeking and refugee children.

A holistic approach to matching

A principal tenet in the care of children is the importance of a child's family background. A child's ethnic origin, culture, language and religion are significant factors to be taken into account when agencies are considering the most appropriate placement for a child; however, such consideration has to take into account *all* the child's needs. Many agencies are well aware that simply identifying a child's ethnic background, while an essential first step in the process, is not sufficient in itself. Adoption agencies will need to go further and think through the implications for the individual child of these cultural factors – how the culture of a family, community and society can influence the way a child sees the world; the significance of religion in a child's daily life; and the importance of maintaining a knowledge of his or her history, culture and language.

What is happening in practice? In relation to the first step of recording "same race placement" considerations, Ivaldi (2000) found practice uneven in his 1998–1999 sample. A key finding was that there was a greater propensity for inner London boroughs (66 per cent) and shire counties (48 per cent) than

others to give special consideration to ethnic matching of the child. Collier remarked in a concluding chapter of Ivaldi's pioneering study that 'it was worrying to see that ethnicity was not identified on Form E as a matching issue for all children and it was noteworthy that transracial adoption seemed to be more likely to take place when this had not been highlighted' (p 113). Clearly, more needs to be done.

The black and minority ethnic children who wait

Back in 1973, the Rowe and Lambert (1973) study, *Children who Wait*, was a turning point in childcare policy and practice. The study identified many delays in the system for all children but of particular interest for this review was the finding that 26 per cent of children waiting for substitute families were black.

Over three decades have passed since then. Black and minority ethnic children continue to wait in care far longer than white children because more black and minority ethnic families are needed. The greatest unmet needs are for families for black boys, older black and Asian children, sibling groups and disabled children from black and Asian backgrounds. Ivaldi's (2000) study found that overall the percentage of black and minority ethnic children waiting for adoption was 17 per cent.

More recent research (Selwyn *et al*, 2004) found that at every age, the process from best interest decision to adoption, took longer for black and Asian children.

BAAF's Be My Parent service aims to find adoptive parents for children whom agencies have been otherwise unable to place. Among those children not in sibling groups, children from black and minority ethnic backgrounds are in the majority. Many are of mixed-heritage and some have heritages that are particularly challenging to find a match for, such as these children whose profiles were featured in June 2006.

> *Robert Ethnic and cultural descent: birth mother: Asian British, Sikh; birth father: black Caribbean (Jamaican), Christian*

> *Primrose Ethnic and cultural descent: birth mother: black African (Somali) and white British; birth father: either Asian Pakistani or black Caribbean.*

The Adoption Register for England and Wales is another family-finding initiative which aims to help agencies find adopters from outside their area when they have not been able to find a local match for them. Most of the children are either in larger sibling groups, are black or of mixed heritage, are older or have special needs (or a combination of these characteristics). Of all the children referred to the Adoption Register in the year 2004–5, 29 per cent were black or of mixed heritage.

Andy Stott, manager of the Adoption Register, says:

> *There is a wide variety of ethnicities and mixes of ethnicity, so sometimes it is a struggle to find an identical match. One of my concerns is that, where black and mixed heritage adopters are concerned, we don't have many families available – and understandably they come with their preferences.*
>
> *Because black and minority ethnic prospective adopters are in short supply, this means, in practice, and in common with the preference of many adopters, that they will be able to adopt babies.*
>
> *We have had quite a few mixed-heritage children, little girls who are two to two-and-a-half years old, who are developing well and making attachments – and they have become "difficult to place". On occasion, families have even turned down children under two years old because they want a younger child.*

Developing identity

Black, Asian and mixed-heritage children who come into care need to grow up with a strong sense of personal and cultural identity in order to prepare them for societal factors they may have to face in childhood and adult life, including racism and discrimination.

The family provides the foundation for building identity. The core of identity is something that is internalised from a range of different factors, including the messages you take on board as you go through life.

Why is identity so important?

- Identity provides us with structure. It is part of our personalities and it is this that equips us with direction and purpose in life as adults.

- Personal identity relates to the way that an individual defines him/herself as different from others. This covers a wide range of factors such as gender, ethnicity, age, culture, religion, sexuality, interests and friends, and is usually multi-faceted.

- For all children, an awareness and understanding of their origins is likely to be important in developing a positive sense of personal identity and self-esteem.

Banks (2002, p157) writes that although all children have an identity development need, some children from some groups are likely to need additional help, in the form of overt intervention, to counter the negative images that may be encountered.

All children who are looked after are vulnerable to negative impacts on their identity formation, resulting from interrupted attachments. Black and minority ethnic children are additionally at risk of disruption of contact with their ethnic group and family of origin. A lack of support for identity formation can lead a child from a black or Asian background to disassociate themselves from their own ethnic group. This may be seen as a coping mechanism, but actually serves to devalue their own sense of self.

Prevatt-Goldstein and Spencer (2000) point out that preparation is also vital for children and black and minority ethnic families in cases where the child is denying his or her racial or cultural heritage.

> *Social workers sometimes say that black adolescents are refusing to live with black people. This is a sad example of the internalisation of the negative messages that society still gives to black people about being black...We do not, however, suggest that such a child should be placed in a black family without proper preparation. This would be setting the child and the family up to fail...A plan of work needs to be undertaken which can help the young person begin to unlock the negative messages they have internalised about black people, their relatives and ultimately themselves. The plan and intervention will depend on the individual children, their ages and their expectations, as well as, most critically, the commitment and understanding of the workers and carers involved. (p 18)*

Hence there is a need for children from black, Asian or mixed backgrounds in the care system, particularly those children who are currently living with families who do not meet their ethnic and cultural needs, to be supported in their placements to develop a positive view of their ethnic and cultural heritage.

A child's culture is essentially what they have lived and known and we all behave the way that we have been socialised. If, however, a black or Asian child has to accept someone else's definition of his or her experience, it will be difficult for that child to discover their own character and to explore and develop their own identity.

Thoburn *et al* (2005) highlighted important messages from minority ethnic children about their need for consistent, skilled, but, above all, caring parenting that provides them with a sense of belonging, boosts their sense of self-worth and competence, and strengthens their pride in their appearance and personalities. In addition, black and Asian young people and others who are visibly different from their carers want their carers to understand the reality of racism and discrimination and they want help in devising strategies to deal with it.

Banks (1995) believes that children are best placed in those families that reflect their own ethnic origin. For the child of mixed parentage, this means that one parent should be black and one white. Banks quotes an 11-year-old boy and nine-year-old girl who were brother and sister of mixed South Asian/white origin, who said: 'We want to know what it would have been like…(to have stayed in a "real" family). We don't want to stand out' (p 24).

As well as providing a strong sense of identity, the black or Asian extended family offers a possibility of a wide network of support and many families still retain strong links overseas. These connections and strengths are rooted in cultural traditions, in the survival of generations in spite of discrimination, and the stresses of migration and, sometimes, persecution.

> *I was quite badly bullied and experienced a lot of racist abuse when I was at school; one of the things that helped me get through it was knowing that I could go home and talk to my parents about it, because they had been through something similar. I hope that won't be the case when Natalie goes to school but I think there are times when you need to identify with someone like you. I came to England from Barbados when I was seven. If it hadn't been for my parents and their friends, I don't think I would have such a balanced sense of self.* (Linda, 35, is from Barbados and has adopted a baby daughter, Natalie. Quoted in Massiah, 2005, p 23)

However, a number of agencies are having enormous difficulty in finding ethnically matched placements for black, Asian and mixed-heritage children, which prompts the question: what happens to these children if there are not suitably matched families?

Transracial placement: the history

Transracial placement or transracial adoption is the term used when a child from one heritage is parented by a family from a different heritage and culture from that of the child.

Small numbers of black children had always been adopted into white families but this became a systematic practice from the late 1960s.

In the mid-1960s, the British Adoption Project was established as an action research project to see if adoptive families could be found for black children in care. During its existence, 53 young black children were placed for adoption with 51 couples. Eighty per cent of those families were white. From this point, right through to the 1970s, transracial adoptions were seen as an appropriate plan for black children needing permanent placements.

During the course of the British Adoption Project, the number of healthy white babies needing adoption in Britain began to fall due to the changes in the law legalising abortion, the advent of the contraceptive pill and the changes in social attitudes that enabled unmarried mothers to keep their children. This meant that many white adopters were prepared to consider adopting black children.

The 1960s also saw the development of the "melting pot" philosophy of race relations, which held that "race" was unimportant and integration was best achieved by mixing up the races and producing (as the singer Madeline Bell put it) 'coffee-coloured people by the score'.

Small (1986) noted that transracial adoptions gained momentum with the philosophy of the assimilation of the immigrant child into society. Singh (2002) stated that the "colour-blind" approach to social work, which precipitated many transracial placements of black children, owed much to the prevalent ideology of the late 1970s and early 1980s. At that time it was believed that black children who identified more closely with white people were actually assimilating successfully; it was seen as a sign of psychological well-being. This assimilationist philosophy was derived from a "cultural deficit" model, which viewed black people as lacking, abnormal or deviant.

At the same time, there was the erroneous belief that black substitute parents could not be found (Small, 1986). There were growing numbers of black children in children's homes at this time, so transracial adoptions were encouraged in order to reduce the number of black children living in institutions.

As Kirton (2000) states, transracial adoption was given its official blessing in the Home Office's *Guide to Adoption Practice* (Home Office, Advisory Council on Child Care, 1970). The guide made no mention of the desirability of "same-race" adoption or the need to recruit black families.

The three main factors that promoted transracial adoptions, according to Kirton (2000), were: the perceived "success" of such adoptions; the continuing shortfall of black adoptive families relative to children in care; and the rise of the "permanency movement" in child care. By the 1970s, transracial adoption had become an established, if doubtless still unusual, practice and black children were mainly placed with white families.

Fostering practice developed in parallel with adoption. Throughout the 1970s, the vast majority of black children were living in institutions. Many others were placed with white foster parents rather than black foster parents.

Black families at that time were disregarded as prospective adopters because they were not seen to correspond to the white stereotypes of an acceptable family. Most childcare agencies of the period did not actively seek to develop methods of recruitment, selection and preparation particularly aimed at increasing the numbers of black substitute parents. When black and minority ethnic families did respond to family-finding publicity, they were likely to face assessment by white social workers and managers whose training and experience at that time would seldom have provided them with the cultural competence to understand and value these families' strengths or to nurture their motivation through the different stages of assessment and preparation through to matching.

Then during the 1980s, ABSWAP (Association of Black Social Workers and Allied Professions) launched a campaign to oppose transracial adoptions. ABSWAP had a growing concern about the failure by authorities to recruit adopters from black and Asian communities, which was leading to children being placed transracially and that this was having a detrimental effect on their development. Kirton (2000, p 21) writes that, in its evidence to the House of Commons Select Committee in 1983, ABSWAP described transracial adoption as 'a microcosm of the oppression of black people in this society', a form of one-way traffic, depriving black communities of their most valuable resources. This contributed to a radical shift in social work practice.

By the late 1980s, the drawbacks of transracial adoptions were coming to light. Children who had been transracially adopted began to share their experiences of facing isolation, their public "visibility" arising from the obvious physical differences between themselves and their adoptive parents and the difficulties they had in developing a coherent picture of who they were or where they belonged. These difficulties had persisted despite the loving care provided by committed adopters. Some transracially placed children were also showing difficulties with cultural identification, a lack of knowledge about their own ethnic heritage, and inadequate skills and strategies for dealing with prejudice and racism.

Gill and Jackson (1983) did a follow-up study on the families that had adopted through the British Adoption Project. When analysing issues related to racial background, the researchers found that the large majority of parents had made only limited attempts to give their children a sense of racial pride and awareness of their racial origin. The children in turn saw themselves as "white" in all but skin colour and had little knowledge or experience of their counterparts growing up in the black community.

> *One strange aspect of my experience is that my upbringing has endowed me with a "white man's mind". I think like a white man even though I am not. I am very sensitive to racism of any kind, but I have had the mind-bending experience of looking at people who have the same features as me and having racist thoughts about them.* (Ron McLay, quoted in *In Search of Belonging: Reflections by transracially adopted people* (Harris (ed), 2006))

Thoburn *et al* (1998) followed up 297 children of minority ethnic origin, who had been placed either transracially or in "matched" families. The researchers concluded that, with appropriate selection and support, white families can successfully parent black children. However, after considering a range of outcome measures such as a positive sense of identity and self-esteem, the researchers advised that, wherever possible, it is desirable to place children with families who are ethnically and culturally similar.

Triseliotis *et al* (2005) quoted critical accounts from some black adults who had been transracially adopted, for example:

> *Racially I felt "apart" as they're white. I got bullied at school about my race and I didn't trust that my adoptive parents really believed I was of equal status to their natural children.* (p 140)

Perlita Harris (2006) edited a collection of pieces from over 50 contributors of all ages who were transracially adopted. The contributors express a range of views about the practice of transracial or transnational adoption, covering adoptive placements made over half a century (between 1950 and 2000) by a number of agencies.

In her introduction, Harris says that many of the experiences described by the contributors challenge any preconceptions that "race" does not matter. She notes that some contributors express gratitude and loyalty to adoptive parents alongside the view that 'if it was not for my adoptive parents I wouldn't have been adopted' and points out:

> *The latter, while it may be true, is not the whole story. Many transracial adoptees (as with the general public) have not asked why there weren't attempts to recruit and assess black adoptive families at the time their placement was made, to question the politics behind transracial and transnational adoption, or to wonder whether there might be viable alternatives to their continued practices.* (p 8)

Transracial placement today

Since the 1980s, there has been a high profile debate about transracial placements and the need for appropriate matching to meet children's cultural and ethnic needs; the importance of ethnically matched placements has been acknowledged for some time. While disagreement remains about how outcomes are conceptualised and measured, there is broad agreement by most researchers that young people require placements that promote their self-esteem and sense of identity and that, wherever possible, this should be with parents who reflect their culture and ethnicity.

The National Adoption Standards for England (Department of Health, 2000b) recommended that a looked after child should be placed in a family that reflects his or her birth heritage, if this can be done without unnecessary delay. UK legislation (see pages 12–14) requires that racial origin, culture, language and religion should be considered when placing children for adoption and fostering. However, in practice, a small number of children are still being placed transracially, with both adoptive and foster families.

> *In relation to the pre- and post-adoption training programmes, the cultural dimensions were virtually absent even when a couple of the adopters had transracial placements. I was a little surprised that transracial placements still existed to the extent that they do.* (Prospective black adopter)

Black, Asian and mixed-heritage children in unmatched foster care placements often end up remaining there permanently because strong attachments have developed and/or repeated family-finding initiatives to achieve a better match have proved unproductive. How are cultural and identity issues addressed for these children if the placement is to continue? Should making the right placement from the moment a child comes into care be a priority? How and when are white foster carers of black, Asian and mixed-heritage children trained, educated and supported? For children who are placed transracially, what is the system to assess the family's "cultural competence"? How rigorous is this assessment? How is the family then supported once the child is placed and afterwards? These challenging questions reflect how preferable it would be to obtain the correct match for a child from the very beginning.

There is also a lack of information about decisions and planning, for black boys in particular, in the absence of matched placements. Detailed analysis of the outcomes for all black, Asian and mixed-heritage children is required. The question is, with limited resources and the need to avoid delay, are agencies' decisions for black children changing? This will come to light when more data are collected on ethnically matched placements. At present, the government does not publish this information.

Racism and discrimination

Barn *et al* (2005) cites racism as a powerful influence in highlighting difference and marginality. The Looked After Children circular (Department of Health, 1998) stresses the significance of racism and the Blueprint Project's *The Care Experience: Through black eyes* report (2004) confirms that black and minority ethnic young people wanted their carers to understand how racism and discrimination affect their development of a positive identity and feeling of self-worth (p 4).

People from black and minority ethnic communities often face a double disadvantage in terms of experiencing poverty and racism. Although equal opportunities legislation has had some success in combating overt discrimination and harassment, indirect discrimination still systematically disadvantages people from black and minority ethnic groups.

The Stephen Lawrence Inquiry produced what has become known as the Macpherson Report (1999). This report acknowledged the existence of "institutional racism" in all major institutions in British society. "Institutional racism" was defined as:

> ...the collective failure of an organisation to provide an appropriate and professional service to people because of their colour, culture and behaviour, which amounts to discrimination through unwitting prejudice, ignorance, thoughtlessness and racist stereotyping which disadvantage minority ethnic people.

A Joseph Rowntree Foundation report (Barn *et al*, 2005) looked at discrimination and service provision and brought together some key issues arising out of research projects supported by the Foundation. Researchers found that services were perceived to cater primarily for white people; minority ethnic people were expected to fit in with existing provision. In terms of access to the services, workers' cultural stereotypes acted as a barrier to minority ethnic people. Services were often viewed as mono-cultural and were found to have some, if not all, of the following characteristics:

- an unrepresentative workforce or no minority ethnic staff;

- limited or non-existent policies and practice guidelines relating to working with minority ethnic users;

- few or no minority ethnic users accessing the service;

- limited relationships with the minority ethnic voluntary sector;

- staff had limited or no awareness or confidence in working with diversity.

Some adoption agencies have implemented measures to combat institutional racism and make their services more accessible to minority ethnic users; all agencies need to keep these issues in mind in relation to the work they do with minority ethnic communities.

Overview of recruitment efforts

As we have seen, historically, through transracial adoption and fostering policies, the message to black and minority ethnic communities has been that they are not valued as adoptive and foster parents for black and minority ethnic children.

The very first attempts to recruit black families for black children were outlined in *The Paid Servant* (1962) by Braithwaite (quoted in Kirton, 2000, p 8), who was later co-opted by the then London County Council to promote efforts to recruit black families.

However, it was a campaign called Soul Kids in 1975 that was the first targeted campaign to recruit black adopters. Both Soul Kids and a number of pilot projects that followed it have demonstrated that targeted campaigns *can* be successful in recruiting adopters from black and Asian communities. For example, there was New Black Families in Lambeth (Small, 1986) and the Khandan project in Scotland (Singh *et al*, 2002). More recently, in 2004, NCH Black Families was set up in London and is also having great success.

NCH London Black Families was developed to meet the needs of the many black and minority ethnic children in the care system; it was commonly felt by local authority and voluntary agencies that it was difficult to recruit appropriate families for the children.

> *By establishing our project which reflects the people that we are working with ethnically, racially and culturally in our team members, management and panel, this has helped families to feel confident in coming forward to us to be considered for adoption. Often when people attend our open days, which we frequently run, or contact us by telephone, they tell us that 'it is like a breath of fresh air' to them; they believe that we will understand their cultures from the outset, which means we can get on with the task of assessing their potential to be adoptive parents, without them feeling that they will have to explain themselves first and foremost!*

> *Building on our work with families and our local authority colleagues has meant that we can carefully consider appropriate matches for*

children and have access to available children throughout the UK.

Our service is racially and culturally sensitive throughout from preparation groups, support groups and social events, meaning that adopters say that they instantly 'feel at home and relaxed'; it has also meant that many of our adopters remain in touch with us after the adoption order and unusually are always willing to lend a hand in terms of advertising, media, making food for our social events and often "pop in" or phone to check out something with us regarding their child in placement, when they are always welcome. They themselves are also highly committed to getting the message out to other potential black adopters.

Many of our adopters have felt anxious about approaching large organisations, or have been put off at the first point of contact; when they have discovered that there is an organisation such as London Black Families, they inform us that they are relieved – 'Finally, an adoption agency for us'. We enable our adopters to come together frequently and especially the men, who are often concerned about the assessment process, to support each other; we never compromise on our high standards and always have the child at the centre of any assessment but believe that we are able to think "out of the box" and support our increasing numbers of adopters through the process. (Jean Smith, Project Manager for NCH Black Families)

Essentially, the recruitment of carers is influenced by an agency's policy, professional practice, budget priorities and the views of potential carers and sometimes birth parents. While many agencies have a "same-race" policy, the evidence on the recruitment of black, Asian and mixed-heritage families demonstrates that it is not always possible to implement it. Many agencies report that their difficulty in recruiting black and Asian carers is having a serious impact and delaying the placement of black, Asian and mixed-heritage children.

The BAAF report, *Acting on Principle* (Barn *et al*, 1997), examined "race" and ethnicity in social services provision for children and families. The report showed that when authorities made genuine efforts to recruit potential carers from minority ethnic backgrounds, they could be successful. From an agency's timely and positive response to an initial enquiry all the way through to assessment and approval, its approach is crucial to the recruitment of

prospective adopters. An insensitive, culturally inappropriate response can cause potential adopters to turn away or to give up entirely.

In order to provide a culturally appropriate response, agencies need to recruit staff from minority ethnic backgrounds. In the NCH study, Selwyn *et al* (2004) found that having staff from black and minority ethnic backgrounds does increase the recruitment and retention of carers and adopters. However, the research also showed that employing more minority ethnic staff was not easy for agencies; even in areas with high minority ethnic populations, agencies had difficulties in recruiting sufficient minority ethnic staff. The study also found that, in spite of advertising and publicity, myths and stereotypes around adoption are still prevalent in minority ethnic communities.

Agencies attempting to widen the pool of available families from black, Asian and mixed-heritage backgrounds need to consider how these myths and stereotypes can be dispelled.

Adoption in my family is seen as a complete no-no. When I told my dad he could not get his head around why I was taking someone else's child. He said that if I wanted a child he would go and get one from Nigeria. When I went to Nigeria with Nathan, no one could believe that I had adopted him because they could not conceive the idea of adopting outside the family. They're all convinced he's my birth child. Our culture, my parents' generation, are really into blood connections. (Bunmi, 37, is Nigerian and has adopted a son, Nathan (quoted in Massiah, 2005, p 45))

In 2001, BAAF asked MORI to conduct a survey of the public's attitudes to adoption, which found that black people are more likely than others to say that they would consider adopting a child some time in the future (48 per cent as opposed to 24 per cent of the white population interviewed). *The Voice* conducted a mini-survey in 2000 to obtain readers' opinions on adoption (Sunmonu, 2000). The newspaper concluded that the lack of take-up within the black community goes further than economic and social barriers. These may sometimes be overcome, but the way applications from black and Asian people are treated is pivotal if more foster carers and adopters are to be recruited.

Therefore, while there may not be a wide pool of available black potential carers, this is not because of any apparent reluctance or unwillingness on the part of these communities. The challenge for agencies is to convert "willingness" into approved carers.

The NCH report recommends that adoption agencies should understand the recruitment process from the black adopters' point of view.

The social worker assigned to us was excellent. She was white and very experienced. She was very professional and concentrated on the main issues. She was different from many of the social workers we had come across in this country who were quite pedantic, over-obsessed with bureaucracy and quite ethno-centric. Our social worker was very friendly, humble and very empowering. (Asian adopters)

Massiah (2005) writes:

Social workers who are culturally aware, open-minded and flexible, who gave accurate information and were honest about what was possible and how long things would take, were key to adopters having a positive experience of the adoption and matching process. (p 5)

Family-finding services

The Adoption Register for England and Wales and the increasing use throughout the UK of regional consortia of adoption agencies means that agencies are sharing more information about adopters and increasing the number of inter-agency placements. By pooling their resources in a consortium, agencies can sometimes increase the chance of finding suitably ethnically matched adopters when they cannot find any locally that match a particular child's needs.

The Adoption Register is successfully making links between black, Asian and mixed-heritage children and suitable adopters from other parts of the country. Only 16 per cent of the prospective adopters referred to the Adoption Register were black or of mixed heritage, yet 56 per cent of the single children successfully placed were black or of mixed heritage. In other words, among the children who were placed singly, the proportion of black and mixed-heritage children placed was higher than the proportion of white children.

There are also other family-finding services such as BAAF's well-established service, *Be My Parent*. All UK local authorities, most voluntary adoption agencies and many hundreds of independent fostering providers are BAAF member agencies. A number of specialist projects involved in the recruitment of black families, such as NCH London Black Families and Barnardo's Jigsaw Project, are also members.

Prospective adopters can subscribe to BAAF's monthly *Be My Parent* newspaper or Adoption UK's *Children Who Wait*, which feature profiles of children waiting to be adopted or fostered long-term.

Be My Parent placed 236 children with an adoptive or permanent foster family in the year 2005–6. This included 93 children from a black or minority ethnic background, who were placed with a total of 41 black or minority ethnic adopters and five black or minority ethnic permanent foster carers.

In a *Be My Parent* subscriber survey in 2004, 599 subscribers defined their ethnicity, of which three per cent were African or Caribbean; 2.7 per cent were Asian; 0.7 per cent were mixed African or Caribbean and white; and 0.5 per cent were mixed Asian and white.

The BAAF/ALG Project

The BAAF/Association of London Government project for recruitment of black minority ethnic carers offered BAAF the opportunity to explore best practice in more detail. The task was to work with London boroughs to increase recruitment of carers from black and minority ethnic communities. The project started in 2002 and has funding until March 2007.

It is co-ordinated by one project worker, who was responding to:

- the Government's target of increasing the number of looked after children adopted from care by 40 per cent and if possible 50 per cent by 2004–5 (Department of Health White Paper, 2000a);

- the evidence that black and minority ethnic children encounter longer delays than their white peers at all stages of the adoption process, or may not be referred for adoption even where this is the most appropriate permanency plan;

- the need to analyse and overcome barriers that prevent more carers from minority communities to be successfully recruited, approved and matched with children waiting for families.

This Good Practice Guide builds on the work of the project by examining some of those barriers and presenting many tried and tested ways of recruiting more carers from black and minority ethnic communities.

3 Legislation and guidance

Promoting racial equality

All children have a range of placement needs. Black and other minority ethnic children should have the same opportunity as most white children of being found an adoptive placement which reflects their own ethnicity and culture.

The legislation on promoting equality and eliminating discrimination means that adoption agencies must provide services that are fair and accessible to everyone, regardless of their ethnicity, religion, language or cultural heritage.

Relevant legislation and guidance that apply throughout the UK include:

- **Article 13 of the European Union Treaty**, which gives the EU powers to take steps to combat discrimination on grounds of sex, race, disability, sexual orientation, age and religion. The UK joined the EU in 1973.

- **The Race Relations Act 1976**. This Act made it unlawful to discriminate against anyone on grounds of race, colour, nationality or ethnic or national origin.

- **Article 14 of the European Convention on Human Rights**. The Human Rights Act 1998 brought the ECHR into force in the UK in October 2000. Article 14, Prohibition of discrimination, states that the enjoyment of the rights and freedoms in the Convention must be secured without discrimination on any ground including race, colour, language, religion and association with a national minority.

- **The Race Relations (Amendment) Act 2000**, introduced in response to the MacPherson Report. This Act goes further and requires named public authorities to review their policies and procedures; to remove discrimination and the possibility of discrimination; and to actively promote race equality. In other words, public authorities are required not only to address unlawful discrimination where it occurs, but also to be pro-active in preventing it from occurring. They must ensure that children, young people and their families are provided with services which promote equality and value diversity. Public services are to be provided in a way that is fair and accessible to all.

- **The Equality Act 2006**. This Act modernises anti-discrimination and equality law, including the promotion of racial equality and will repeal parts of the 1976 and 2000 Acts when it is fully in force.

Ensuring continuity for children

It is not only in the UK that the importance of continuity for children was recognised during the 1980s. The United Nations Convention on the Rights of the Child (1989) provides a context for domestic law. Britain is a signatory to the Convention, which outlines the rights of all children everywhere. Article 20 (3) states that, when considering placement solutions for a child, due regard shall be paid to the desirability of continuity in a child's upbringing and to the child's ethnic, religious, cultural and linguistic background.

As we have seen, the climate in the UK was changing in the 1980s; the assimilationist philosophy fell from favour and the importance of ethnic identity and continuity in children's cultural and religious traditions and language was recognised. Legislation was put in place for England, Wales, Scotland and Northern Ireland with the aim of protecting children's right to have these factors considered.

England and Wales

The Children Act 1989, Section 22, Part III places a duty on local authorities, in relation to children looked after by them, to give due consideration to the child's racial origin, culture, linguistic background and religious persuasion. This means that agencies need to attract as carers 'not only people of different ethnic backgrounds but also people of diverse religions and those whose first language is not English' (Frazer and Selwyn, 2005).

This Act constituted an important political shift in social policy for looked after children: for the first time it became unlawful to ignore a child's "race", language, culture and religion. The Act also stressed that children need to be helped to remain within their own communities.

The Government circular (LAC 98 (20) *Adoption: Achieving the right balance*), issued in 1998, had a section called 'Understanding the needs of children from black and minority ethnic communities'. This circular states the importance of ethnic and cultural matching and recruitment of suitable families but stresses that the overriding need is to find adoptive parents for the child. It does not rule out transracial adoption.

> *A child's ethnic origin, culture, language and religion are significant factors to be taken into account when adoption agencies are considering the most appropriate placement for a child; however, such consideration has to take into account all the child's needs...Where no family can be identified which matches significantly to the child's ethnic origin and cultural heritage, the adoption agency's efforts to find an alternative suitable family must be proactive and diligent. The Government has made it clear that it is unacceptable for a child to be denied loving adoptive parents solely on the grounds that the child and adopters do not share the same racial or cultural background.* (Department of Health, 1998, pp 3–4)

A further Government letter, CI (2000) 7 (Social Services Inspectorate, Department of Health, 2000) was issued in response to the way local authority social services departments had implemented the earlier circular. It emphasises the need to seek adopters from minority ethnic communities:

> *Specific recruitment campaigns directed at minority ethnic communities are needed; we have no reason to believe that targeting minority ethnic communities will meet with anything but an encouraging response.* (p 9)

In 2000, the Department of Health White Paper, *Adoption: A new approach*, set a target of increasing the number of children adopted from care by 40 per cent and, if possible, 50 per cent by 2004–5.

The National Adoption Standards (Department of Health, 2000) recommend that the family of choice for a looked after child is one that reflects his or her birth heritage, provided this can be done without "unnecessary delay".

The Adoption and Children Act 2002 re-emphasised the need for ethnically matched placements in adoption. Section 1 provides a welfare checklist for adoption and placement order proceedings and states that, in placing a child for adoption, the adoption agency must give due consideration to the child's religious persuasion, racial origin and linguistic background. This Act also provides a new framework for adoption support, including a new right to an assessment for adoption support needs, and detailed regulations covering the payment of financial support to adoptive parents. The statutory guidance in *Every Child Matters – Change for Children* (2003) outlines the roles and responsibilities of the Director of Children's Services (DCS) and Lead Member (LM) for Children's Services. The DCS and LM must have due regard to the local authority's responsibilities to promote equality of opportunity and good race relations and eliminate discrimination.

On the subject of recruitment and matching, the National Minimum Standards for Voluntary Adoption Agencies and Local Authority Adoption Services in England and Wales (Department of Health, 2003) include the following:

> *The adoption agency has a written plan for the implementation and evaluation of effective strategies to recruit sufficient adopters to meet the needs of the range of children waiting for adoption locally.*

> *Children are matched with adopters who best meet their assessed needs. Wherever possible, this will be with a family which reflects their ethnic origin, cultural background, religion and language...*

Where this cannot be done:

> *...the adoption agency makes every effort to find an alternative suitable family within a realistic timescale to ensure the child is not left waiting indefinitely in the care system.*

Scotland

The duties of local authorities in Scotland are similar to those in England and Wales.

- The Adoption (Scotland) Act 1978 in Section 6 (1) imposes a duty on courts and adoption agencies to have regard, so far as practicable, to the child's religious persuasion, racial origin and cultural and linguistic background 'in reaching any decision relating to the adoption of the child'.

- The Children (Scotland) Act 1995, Section M (4), places duties on local authorities to have regard, so far as practicable, to the child's religious persuasion, racial origin and cultural and linguistic background when making any decision concerning a child they are or may be looking after and when providing services for children in need. The Guidance for adoption issued under the 1995 Act (Scottish Office, 1997, Vol 3) highlights the need to identify all aspects of a child's heritage and to plan placement and recruitment on the basis of matching a child's placement with his/her heritage (Chapter 1, paragraphs 10 and 11). The Guidance for fostering (Scottish Office, 1997, Vol 2) also mentions issues of diversity (Chapter 3, paragraphs 14, 27, 28, 63, and 83).

The National Care Standards for Adoption Agencies (Scottish Executive, 2005) state in the introduction:

Placing agencies must try to meet the child's ethnic, cultural, faith and language needs. Individual agencies may not have a wide enough range of families available for all children and must work together to share resources.

Standards for children include:

The family that is chosen for you reflects as closely as possible your ethnic and cultural background and your faith. Other important things that are taken into consideration are where the family live, family composition, lifestyle, qualities of your prospective adopter and your views. (Standard 5.2)

Standards for prospective adopters include:

You know about a child's ethnic, cultural, faith, language, emotional, health and developmental needs and potential future needs. (Standard 27.1)

In contrast, the National Care Standards for foster care and family placement services (Scottish Executive, 2005) have less provision, although the introduction includes equality and diversity as part of the main principles.

Standards for children and young people include:

You know the agency makes sure your foster carer:
Understands the implications of your culture or faith. (Standard 2.6)
You can be confident that your identity and self-esteem will be valued and promoted. (Standard 3)
You know that the agency prepares and helps your foster carer to respect and understand issues of diversity, including sexuality and lifestyle choices. (Standard 3.3)

Northern Ireland

Similarly, the legislation in Northern Ireland requires agencies to take these factors into account but it has a greater focus on religion.

- The Adoption Order (NI) 1987, as amended, enables a freeing order to be made subject to a parental requirement as to the child's religious upbringing. Article 16(1)(b)(i) enables the court to grant an adoption order 'subject to a condition with respect to the religious persuasion in which the child is to be brought up'.

- The Children (NI) Order 1995, Article 52(6) requires that, while a care order is in force, the authority shall not 'cause the child to be brought up in any religious persuasion other than that in which he would have been brought up if the order had not been made'.

- The Children (NI) Order 1995 Guidance and Regulations require that, when providing services for children in need and when planning for a child in care, the Trust should take into account and consider the child's 'religious persuasion, racial origin, cultural and linguistic background...' and any other particular needs of the child (in relation to health, development, education, physical and/or sensory disability or learning disability).

The legislative requirements of the four countries in the UK, then, make it obligatory for placement agencies to address holistically the needs of black and minority ethnic children within an equality and diversity framework.

4 Brief overview of research

There have been a number of research studies on black and minority ethnic children's sense of ethnic and racial identity and the effects of transracial adoption. The research which this guide draws on is mainly from the UK. A key message from these studies, endorsed by nearly all researchers, is that ethnic matching is important in meeting the identity and cultural needs of black and minority ethnic children (see Chapter 2, *The context*). There is also clear evidence that black and minority ethnic children are over-represented in the care system and that more black and minority ethnic adoptive parents and foster carers are needed.

Understandably, there is continuing concern about how black and minority ethnic carers can be recruited in greater numbers. The study commissioned by NCH (Selwyn *et al*, 2004) looked at agency policy and practice in terms of recruiting black, Asian and black mixed-parentage adopters and made recommendations. The authors expressed surprise that, despite previous "good practice" guidance from BAAF and the Thomas Coram Adoption Service (in 1991 in both cases), which had stressed the importance of staff awareness, of reaching out and communicating with minority communities, and of providing a sensitive and responsive service, more minority ethnic applicants had not been recruited. Somehow the message was not getting through.

Among the obstacles to recruitment of black and minority ethnic carers that have been identified, the NCH and other surveys point to the economic and material disadvantage experienced by black and minority ethnic groups in the UK, cultural barriers, institutional racism and a real feeling among black minority ethnic families that they are not valued as carers (see Chapter 6, *Black and minority ethnic communities*).

Population trends may also increase recruitment difficulties:

> *...the very young age profiles of the mixed-parentage, Pakistani and Bangladeshi communities, and of the Muslim and Sikh communities, may place children from these communities at a relative disadvantage in terms of the number of adults available to them as potential adopters...*

> *...The difficulties which local authorities report in identifying ethnically matched adopters for children of mixed parentage are perhaps unsurprising when one considers, for example, that in 2001 the ratio of children to adults aged 30–39 years of mixed white/black Caribbean parentage was 1 to 0.2, and the ratio of children to adults of mixed white/black African parentage, mixed white/Asian parentage and any other mixed parentage was 1 to 0.3.* (Frazer and Selwyn, 2005)

The NCH study draws attention not only to the importance of local authorities having good information on the ethnicity, language, and culture of the children they are looking after (this still cannot be assumed to be in place in all authorities) but that the information needs to be collated and analysed to help plan recruitment as effectively as possible.

As they comment:

> *The lack of analysis of information could lead to scarce resources being wasted on, for example, poorly targeted advertising...managers within adoption agencies need far better information systems and ones they can access directly...* (Selwyn *et al*, 2004)

A recurrent message from all these studies is the need to avoid stereotypical views or unwarranted assumptions regarding prospective minority ethnic carers and their varying family patterns. For example, as Frazer and Selwyn point out, it might be assumed that more black and minority ethnic children are looked after in kinship care and that this explains their under-representation in adoption. However, a recent study suggested this is not the case:

> *Significantly more black and minority ethnic children (60%) were placed with unrelated carers than were living with family and friends (40%). This is different to the situation in the*

United States. It may be that black and minority ethnic parents are less successful in coming to the attention of social workers when decisions about care are being made or that fewer are in a position to provide care. (Farmer and Moyers, (undated))

Fortunately, there are a number of examples of good practice in agencies and specialised projects around the UK which have been successful in recruiting black and minority ethnic carers.

In later chapters, we provide a sequence of snapshots of successful practice within particular regions, consortia and agencies, and thereby hope to promote increased awareness of the factors which contribute to success in recruitment (Chapter 7, *What works?*)

5 Policy and practice

As we have seen, legislation in all the countries of the UK recognises the importance of considering a child's cultural, linguistic, racial and religious background when placing him or her in a new family. Adoption agencies follow this practice in the belief that it will give the child a better chance of developing a positive sense of identity and self-esteem. They also recognise that it can help children who are trying to cope with prejudice and racism as they grow up in British society.

However, finding a suitable ethnically matched family can also be a long and difficult process and, while doing everything possible to find a family that is ethnically matched, social workers are also required to take into account the effect of delay on the child's wellbeing.

Agencies should have a clear policy regarding ethnic matching, which should refer to the question of delay in meeting a child's need for a permanent family. They also need specific recruitment strategies to attract prospective adopters and foster carers from varying ethnic groups and cultures to meet the needs of the children in their care.

Phillips (2000) analysed the extent to which local authorities had considered the needs of black and minority ethnic children in their Quality Protects Management Action Plans (MAPs). She found a great deal of variation in the extent to which the needs of black and minority ethnic looked after children are recognised and responded to. The study found that, although some local authorities did provide an ethnic breakdown of foster carers, few MAPs provided detailed information as to the extent of placement matching in terms of ethnicity.

A large percentage of local authorities stated that they wanted to increase the number of black and minority ethnic foster carers. For those that set this as a target, there were a range of responses, varying from some with just a generalised intention to achieve a greater percentage of black and minority ethnic carers, to those authorities which had a more detailed plan with specific steps as to how this objective would be realised. Interestingly, it was not always the authorities which had the larger percentages of black children and families within their locality or even those that had the larger percentage of black and minority ethnic children in the looked after system that had the most well developed strategies for achieving this objective.

On the issue of adoption for black and minority ethnic children, there were three main responses from local authorities:

- undertaking an analysis of need of children awaiting adoption;

- targeting recruitment campaigns aimed specifically at black and minority ethnic communities with the aim of increasing the pool of black and minority ethnic carers;

- appointing a worker to increase the number of black and minority ethnic adoptive carers.

Although local authorities could supply figures on the ethnicity of children awaiting adoption, the accuracy and detail of these figures differed greatly. Some local authorities did provide some more detailed information on placements in relation to the ethnic breakdown of children and carers, and a few said that they had achieved ethnic matching for placements.

Phillips also noted that 87 per cent of local authorities adopted a "colour-blind" approach to the needs of black children who are disabled, i.e. that needs arising from their ethnic and cultural identities were not given consideration.

Case studies

A large local authority in south-east England

The Adoption Team Manager says:

> *The agency does try very hard to match children with adopters of the same ethnicity. If we do not have any suitable adopters, I will authorise inter-agency funding in order that we can widen our search. However, no child should have to wait indefinitely for the ideal placement. We also have to take account of children's other needs such as health, contact issues and background factors*

and over-riding everything is whether the adopters can offer a stable and secure placement to a child. Whilst the Government circular LAC 98(20) has now been superseded, it was a very helpful document and one to which I still refer!

We haven't got a policy that says in so many words that, when necessary, we will place children transracially. However, where we are unable to recruit adopters of the same ethnicity, we will consider transracial placements with "culturally aware" families and have placed children in such circumstances.

It is becoming increasingly difficult to match children with families of the same ethnicity due to children's diverse and complex racial backgrounds, for instance, currently we are family-finding for two children who are Jamaican/Indian/White British who have foetal valproate syndrome, a child who is white British/Afghani Muslim with an eating disorder and a child of white Eastern European (Albanian) descent.

Kirklees Metropolitan Council

Kirklees Metropolitan Council serves the Yorkshire Pennines area. Lynrose Kirby, Adoption Team Manager, says:

We aim to place black and minority children with families which match their own ethnic backgrounds as closely as possible (as we do with white British children). The majority of black and minority ethnic children we need to place are from a mixed Pakistani Muslim and white British background. We generally also have one or two children from African or African-Caribbean and White British culture to place per year.

We are generally successful in matching children with an adoptive family of the same ethnic background but have to accept that, in order to do this, we often have to use interagency placements and may have to wait a considerable period of time to achieve this match and that there are financial implications.

We do usually manage to adhere to our "same-race" policy. The exceptions to this tend to be foster carers who have had a transracial placement, who then subsequently apply to adopt the child.

If we cannot find a match with a black or minority ethnic family for a child, then we would look to place with a white family who could demonstrate strong links with the black or minority ethnic community, a good understanding of the issues for the child and a commitment to meet the child's cultural needs.

We could do with a stronger presence in terms of African-Caribbean families. We also struggle to place children who have more complicating factors such as black and minority ethnic children with a mental health background of schizophrenia or a disability.

North London Adoption Consortium

The London boroughs of Barnet, Camden, Enfield, Haringey and Islington, together with two voluntary adoption agencies, Norwood and Parents for Children, form the North London Adoption Consortium. The consortium does not have policies of its own on placement; each agency has its own policy.

Agencies meet regularly to share information about waiting children and available applicants and try to identify suitable placements for children. Consortium members also arrange joint training and recruitment drives and make places available on each other's preparation groups so that applicants do not have to wait too long to join a group.

Between meetings, social workers send publicity material with children's profiles and photographs to the consortium's Development Co-ordinator, who circulates them to all the member agencies.

The consortium carries out some joint recruitment activities. In 2005 it organised an Adoption Exchange Day in Islington, to which it invited four other London consortia and the Adoption Register. Seventy approved adopters from over 20 statutory and voluntary adoption agencies attended.

Marion Hundleby, Development Co-ordinator, says:

The details of over 100 families and children are circulated through the consortium in a year – around 75 children and 25 adoptive families.

The children for whom consortium members are seeking families are of several ethnicities and mixed ethnicity, but the biggest identified need is for West African families, particularly for boys. Some children have very mixed heritages – sometimes three or four heritages for one child. A lot of the children have a black heritage but there are also many who are Mediterranean and East

European. We also have some children who are Vietnamese or Somalian, communities that are not particularly numerous or settled in this part of London.

If we had a West African child we were struggling to place, we might place them in an African-Caribbean family – which is not ideal, but would at least address the issues of the child's "visibility" and helping to deal with racism.

In this area we have very few children of Indian heritage who need adoption. When we have Asian parents, especially if they are Hindu, we struggle to place children with them. We do use the Adoption Register and offer it the families that we can't use. It is important to increase the pool of adopters – but the reality is that, in the consortium, we are all fishing in the same pool. All the local authorities need adopters from black and minority ethnic communities or of mixed ethnicities. That produces a certain tension. Some consortia require their member agencies to put all their approved adopters in the pool very quickly, but in ours we first look at whether we go with each other or not.

We have regular team managers' meetings so that we can talk about children and prospective adopters who are coming through the process.

The London borough of Tower Hamlets

Namita Singh, Team Manager for the permanent placement team, says:

We don't have a policy but we have a protocol: we make the best match possible in the timescale laid down in the national guidelines.

In the first six months we would try to find as close a match as possible. Tower Hamlets is a very small borough and we have very few children who can be placed within the borough so we start looking interagency immediately. We belong to the North-East London Adoption Consortium and we use each others' families quite well, but it could be improved. We have a mailing list of all the fostering and adoption agencies and if we have permission to feature a child, we do a profile and run it on that. We give it to the Adoption Register as well.

When we know we will find it difficult, we start looking for a family as soon as we can; for instance, we have a three-year-old Kenyan black girl whose mother is having episodes of mental ill-health. At an early stage we initiate care

proceedings and start looking for a family at the same time.

If a child has been waiting longer than six months, we would go back to the panel and say that we need to widen the search and consider a family of a different ethnicity. Tower Hamlets is interesting because we have the fastest growing Bangladeshi population but, in line with the trend among the Asian population, the children are not over-represented in care. We have between 40 and 60 children to place each year for adoption or permanent fostering. Around 10 of them may be Asian but they would tend to be the older children or teenagers, for whom adoption may not be the plan. Most children are of mixed-heritage, African-Caribbean or African origin or older white children. But trends change. This year we have had more younger Asian children than usual. Tower Hamlets is a borough with a high transient population, and the population profile changes.

A large proportion of the birth parents are drug users and have issues around mental health, which complicates matters.

Black adopters are in short supply and they can be choosy about the children they take. Even with a little baby, we may have to search quite hard for adoptive parents if the birth mother is a drug user or has a history of mental health problems.

We do occasionally make transracial placements where one child is white and has a sibling of mixed parentage – we might place them with a white single parent who has a wide network of black friends and lives in a multicultural area. The other way a transracial placement might happen is when a foster carer looks after the child and wants to adopt – then it is very difficult to move that child on. You have to make sure there is training for the carer, and support for the carer and the child.

We can be flexible about allowances. For instance, we have a black boy who has attention deficit hyperactivity disorder (ADHD) and autism and finding a family for him would be very difficult. His foster carer wanted to adopt him but couldn't do so without the fostering allowance. So we gave her an enhanced adoption allowance and are arranging respite care to cover the school holidays.

In terms of principle, we are committed to "same race" placements – but I think it is a fallacy that we would be able to place all our children if we were prepared to match them with adoptive parents of other ethnicities. There are not enough adopters to go round and in the current climate we would always struggle to place older children and children with special needs.

A county council in the Midlands

The Adoption Team Manager considers that the county council's adoption team is fairly successful in placing black and minority ethnic children in suitable adoptive families. She says the key is to look at where children are in the legal process and start seeking a suitable family early on, looking within the regional area on an interagency basis if the agency does not have any suitable approved families itself. It usually approves three or four black/minority ethnic households each year as adopters; it also belongs to an adoption consortium.

The minority ethnic children who need adoptive families are mainly African-Caribbean or mixed white and African-Caribbean. The adoption team's policy is that, wherever possible, it will try to match children with adoptive families who reflect their ethnicity, but if this is not achievable within around six months, it will consider other options such as placing them with a white family. However, it can usually find black and minority ethnic adopters for the children who need them, and there have been no transracial adoptions for the last seven years.

The main issue for the adoption team is how best to meet the needs of mixed-heritage children – they are over-represented in the care system locally and yet the number of prospective adoptive families of mixed ethnicity is limited. Mixed-heritage children are placed with a black family or a black single adopter if no suitable mixed-heritage family can be found.

The adoption service does not do much recruitment advertising. It prioritises applications from black and minority ethnic people, which means that if their application is accepted, they can attend preparation groups and be assessed sooner than others. It will accept people from outside the county if they are black or from a minority ethnic group. This is related to its policy of having a choice of families – the aim is to have the option of two or three families for a child if possible.

All the county council's services have to carry out an equality impact assessment, looking at their policies and procedures and how they impact on ethnic minorities. One issue that was highlighted for the adoption service was the amount and complexity of written material that prospective adopters need to read and forms that they need to complete. If necessary, information can be translated into different languages and interpreters can be brought in for people attending adoption preparation groups. As well as the basic adoption allowance, extra allowances are payable, depending on the needs of the child.

The county council aims to recognise and celebrate children's cultural heritages, and there is a worker who works with all children in care, and their carers, to help ensure their racial and cultural needs are met and to help provide resources and support.

Black and minority ethnic communities living in Britain

History

Black people have been migrating to and living in Britain for centuries. Small black communities began to grow around the docksides of Canning Town (London), Liverpool and Cardiff before the First World War. During the Second World War, many black servicemen from the army, navy and air force and also wartime workers arrived in Britain to help the war effort.

It was not until the late 1950s and 1960s that the black and Asian presence began to increase in Britain. Commonwealth countries such as India and particularly English-speaking Caribbean islands such as Jamaica gave Britain the much-needed workers to rebuild the post-war economy and provide a labour force for hospitals, factories, bus companies and railways. Many had high expectations of what England would offer them but found that housing was in short supply and that black people were not accepted by many of the white British population.

Many of those who came over to pave the way for their families to join them had to leave their children behind in the care of their extended family. When children came over later, it made the housing situation even more difficult; it was not unusual for landlords to evict families if children joined them.

Hong Kong Chinese, too, arrived in Britain in large numbers through the 1950s to work in the restaurant business. They mostly settled in London but many settled in Manchester and there were small concentrations in other cities.

The Commonwealth Immigration Act 1962 placed restrictions on immigration from Commonwealth countries and these have been tightened by successive governments.

In the two years before this Act, substantial numbers of women and children, especially from Asia, took the opportunity to enter the country to join the men who had already settled here. The second and third generation descendants of those post-war immigrants – black, Asian and Chinese – now form part of large and established communities in the UK.

In recent years, the pattern of immigration has changed. People have come to the UK – and continue to come – from various countries to work, to study, to seek asylum or to escape economic hardship in their countries of origin. Newer communities have formed, such as Somali, Eritrean and Kurdish communities.

Home Office immigration figures show that, of people settling in the UK in 2004, 32 per cent were from Africa and 21 per cent from the Indian sub-continent. Since 2004, nationals of Eastern European countries such as Poland and the Czech Republic have also been coming in larger numbers to settle in the UK.

Minority ethnic population

The 2001 Census (Office for National Statistics, 2002) reveals that 7.9 per cent of the UK population – 4.6 million people – are from a non-white ethnic group.

- Indians were the largest minority group at 1.8 per cent
- Pakistanis were the next largest at 1.3 per cent
- People from mixed ethnic backgrounds made up 1.2 per cent
- Black Caribbeans made up 1 per cent
- Black Africans made up 0.8 per cent

The 2001 Census was the first census to have "mixed" as a category under ethnic profile. The two largest sub-groups were white and black Caribbean, and white and Asian.

The "mixed" group had the youngest age profile, with 55 per cent under the age of 16. The Bangladeshi group also had a young age profile, with 38 per cent under 16 and 35 per cent of Pakistanis under the age of 16. Only 19 per cent of white UK citizens were under 16, while the white group has the highest proportion (16 per cent) of people aged 65 and over (White, 2002).

Two per cent of Scotland's population is from a black or mixed-heritage background: 70 per cent of the black and mixed-heritage population are classified as

Asian, that is, Pakistani, Bangladeshi, Chinese or other South Asian, with Pakistanis being the largest group at 31 per cent (General Register Office for Scotland, 2003).

Religion

With reference to religion in the UK, the 2001 Census found that:

- 72 per cent of people said that their religion was Christian

- Nearly 3 per cent describe their religion as Muslim

- The next largest groups were Hindus (1 per cent), Sikhs (0.6 per cent), Jewish (0.5 per cent) and Buddhist (0.3 per cent).

- Majorities of black people and those from mixed ethnic backgrounds identified themselves as Christian (71 per cent and 52 per cent respectively).

In terms of numbers of black and minority ethnic people from different faiths:

- There were 815,000 black Christians

- There were 353,000 Christians from mixed ethnic backgrounds

- Pakistani Muslims (686,000)

- Indian Hindus (471,000)

- Indian Sikhs (307,000)

- Bangladeshi Muslims (261,000)

Around 14 per cent of people in the Black Caribbean group, the "Other Black" group and the mixed ethnic groups chose not to answer the religion question in the Census – almost twice the average for Great Britain as a whole.

The Indian group was the most religiously diverse, with 45 per cent Hindu, 29 per cent Sikh and a further 13 per cent Muslim. In contrast, the Pakistani and Bangladeshi groups were more homogeneous, with Muslims accounting for 92 per cent of each ethnic group.

In terms of religion, the 2001 Census showed that 23 per cent of those from mixed ethnic backgrounds stated that they had no religion, compared with 15 per cent of the British population as a whole.

Localities

Black and Asian communities are clustered in Britain's major cities and conurbations. Settlement patterns have taken some groups to certain parts of the country, for example, there are Pakistani concentrations in the Midlands and the north, which have also influenced employment outcomes.

The 2001 Census (Office for National Statistics, 2002) shows that 47.6 per cent of all people from minority ethnic communities live in Greater London and 13.6 per cent live in the West Midlands. Smaller concentrations are found in Yorkshire and Humberside, in the north-west and in Merseyside.

In terms of where different ethnic groups are most likely to live:

- 78 per cent of black Africans live in London

- 61 per cent of black Caribbeans live in London

- 54 per cent of Bangladeshis live in London

- 70 per cent of people of mixed ethnicity live in London

In contrast, Pakistanis are more dispersed, with 19 per cent in London, 21 per cent in the West Midlands, 20 per cent in Yorkshire and Humberside and 20 per cent in the north-west.

London's diversity

In an overview in *The Guardian* of the capital's growing diversity (21 January 2005), Benedictus pointed out that the people of London speak more than 300 languages and the city has at least 50 non-indigenous communities with a population of 10,000 or more. Virtually every other "race", nation, culture and religion in the world can claim at least a handful of Londoners.

Different communities tend to live in different areas of London, and knowing where to find these communities is important if agencies need to target families with particular ethnic or religious backgrounds. For instance, London's south-Asian community has settled in various parts of the city but there is a predominance of certain religions in certain areas. In general terms, the Sikh Punjabis are located in Southall and south-east London, the Hindu Gujeratis live in north-west London and the Muslim Bangladeshis live in Tower Hamlets. South London is said to have more black Caribbean and black African communities.

Education

The Annual Local Area Labour Force Survey data for 2001–2 looked at educational qualifications in Great Britain. The results show the following.

- The ethnic groups with the highest proportions of people with degrees or higher educational qualifications were the Black African, Chinese and Indian groups.

- The ethnic groups with the lowest proportion of people with such higher level qualifications were the Bangladeshi and Pakistani groups.

- The ethnic groups with the highest proportion of people with no educational qualifications were the Bangladeshi (44 per cent) and Pakistani (34 per cent) groups.

A lack of educational qualifications clearly has implications for employment prospects and income.

Employment and income levels

In general terms, black and minority ethnic groups tend to have lower levels of economic activity than their white counterparts.

The Economic and Social Research Council Facts and Figures report (29 March 2006) that the employment rate for ethnic minorities in Great Britain in 2002 was 59 per cent compared to an overall rate of 75 per cent. This gap has been consistent for the last 20 years. The 2001 Census highlights that minority ethnic households are more likely to have lower incomes than white households.

Despite government efforts and a legislative framework specifically directed to support black and minority ethnic communities, members of some of these communities are more likely than white people to live in low income households. The National Statistics Ethnicity report on Low Income states that Pakistanis and Bangladeshis were much more likely than other groups to be living on low incomes – 68 per cent were living in low-income households after housing costs were deducted.

Among men, those from black Caribbean, black African, Bangladeshi and mixed ethnic groups had the highest unemployment rates (between 13 and 14 per cent), according to the Office of National Statistics (National Statistics Online). These rates were around three times the rates for white British men.

While family generations and geography play their part, many Asian groups are characterised by the low work participation rates among women. In 2004, Pakistani women had the highest unemployment rates in Great Britain, at 20 per cent (National Statistics Online). Unemployment rates for black Caribbean women (9 per cent) and Indian women (8 per cent) were around twice the rates for white British women.

There are distinctions to be made within the Asian group: the Indians are achieving higher employment rates and occupational advancement than the Pakistanis and the Bangladeshis, as well as higher work participation rates amongst women. From an economic perspective, Indians and Chinese are, on the whole, doing well and sometimes out-performing the white population in schools and in the labour market.

Among those in work, there are only small differences in average pay and occupational achievement between the Black African group and white people. But other minority ethnic groups, from Pakistan, Bangladesh and the Caribbean, for instance, are disadvantaged in the labour markets on a broad range of measurements including achievement, employment rates, earnings, progression and occupational attainment in the workplace, and levels of self-employment. The extent of these disadvantages has fluctuated over time but has not been eliminated. Class, culture and family patterns also play a part in employment choices.

However, even when differences in educational attainment are accounted for, people from minority ethnic groups do not easily get the jobs that they are qualified for. There are various reasons for this. Racism and discrimination are the most obvious factors; however, there are other contributing circumstances. In some cases, minority ethnic communities are concentrated in areas of deprivation. These areas have barriers such as poor public transport and isolation, with high proportions of workless households that may disproportionately affect whole communities. Health can also play an important part. The over-representation of Black Caribbeans, especially males in mental health services, has become evident in health service data. Black people are three times more likely to be diagnosed as having schizophrenia than other users and less likely to be given counselling (Cabinet Office Scoping Note, July 2001).

The Performance and Innovation Unit Ethnic Minorities Economic Performance report (April 2001) refers to the Trade Union Congress report (2000) that showed that racism continues to be a major barrier at work for black and Asian employees, unfairly limiting career progression and development once in employment and that the ethnic gap widened between 1992 and 1999.

Family size

The Labour Force Survey (Office for National Statistics, 2002) showed that Asian households tend to be larger than those from other ethnic groups. Bangladeshi households were the largest, followed by Pakistanis and Indians. Households may contain three generations, with grandparents living with a couple and their children.

More than half of families with dependent children headed by a person of mixed origin (62 per cent) or by a black Caribbean person (54 per cent) were lone parent families.

Both of these factors – large family size and being a single parent – could impact on people's ability to adopt and perhaps also on some agencies' perception of their suitability as adoptive parents.

The implications

As we have seen, the percentage of black and minority ethnic children in the care system is higher than the percentage of black and minority ethnic people in the general population, so proportionally more families are needed from a smaller pool.

Minority ethnic communities tend to cluster in certain cities and towns of the UK. An agency in an area with few people from minority ethnic communities is faced with an uphill task when trying to find a match for a black or Asian child. Even where there are minority ethnic communities in the area, finding people in the right age bracket from specific ethnic backgrounds or combinations of ethnic background can be a challenge. For instance, there may be large numbers of people of Pakistani or Bangladeshi origin in a certain area but the age profile of these groups shows that a substantial percentage of them will be young and not in a position to consider adoption.

Finding families with two parents of different heritages can be particularly difficult as the pool is small. The last Census showed that inter-ethnic marriage is relatively rare: just two per cent (219,000) of all marriages were between people from different ethnic backgrounds (although of course people do not have to be married to adopt, and since s.50 of the Adoption and Children Act 2002 was implemented, two people who are not married and who are living as partners, from opposite sexes or the same sex, 'in an enduring family relationship' can adopt as a couple).

Of these marriages, the most common (26 per cent) were between white and mixed-heritage people. The next most common marriages (15 per cent) were between a white person and someone who described their ethnic group as "other". White and black Caribbean marriages made up 12 per cent and white and Indian marriages 11 per cent.

We have seen how black and Asian families experience social and economic disadvantage. Social workers and policy makers must be aware of the impact both of demographic factors, such as age profile and family size, and of social and economic factors which can act as barriers to adoption.

Some of the newer minority ethnic groups are transient and have not established such large and settled communities as those which have been in this country for generations. Some communities are largely made up of people who have come to the UK to seek asylum; many people do not even have stable immigration status and will be living in rented or insecure accommodation. In some groups there is a skewed population profile, with the population consisting predominantly of young, single males. Factors such as these clearly affect the ability and readiness of people from that community or country to consider adoption.

Barriers to recruitment

The over-representation of black and minority ethnic children in the care system might lead professionals to think that not enough black and ethnic minority carers come forward to foster or adopt. However, this is not necessarily the case; *there are many who want to foster or adopt but are obstructed by circumstances.*

Families do come forward but many are prevented from proceeding because of environmental factors such as income and housing. Factors such as these have tended to disadvantage black and minority ethnic families not only in terms of their availability to adopt, but also in the ways that local authorities perceive and value them.

Income and housing

The main areas of concern centre on accommodation and income. Families may lack the available space required by social services departments. The NCH study (Selwyn et al, 2004) pointed out that adoption practice has to respond to the prevalence within minority ethnic communities of large family sizes, poverty, poor housing and language barriers.

> *I have already adopted a five-year-old son and we live in a two-bedroom council flat. I approached my agency to adopt another child and was told that I did not have enough room. They didn't even bother to ask anything else. How many families can provide an extra room? I shared a room with my sisters when I was growing up. Why is that not acceptable?* (Black adopter)

In many cases families have a history of children sharing a room, which is their cultural norm.

There is also the financial cost of bringing up a child. If nearly 40 per cent of black and minority ethnic families earn less than the average wage, then it is unlikely that they will have the financial means to look after an extra child without some financial support being made available (CRE, 2005).

Following the Adoption and Children Act 2002, all adopters in England and Wales can be assessed for financial support. Allowances and grants are also available in Scotland. Agencies should ensure they get across the message about adoption allowances and other support, for instance, for adapting or extending homes or even rehousing adoptive families who can take sibling groups, and have policies in place to deliver the resources needed when families come forward.

Cultural barriers

Agencies need to be aware of cultural differences in attitudes to adoption and to social worker involvement.

> *We have a culture of looking after each other's and other people's children, sometimes for years, with no social recognition, no financial assistance and no assessment process... The thing that stops many other black people from*

> *adopting is tied up with the assessment process. Within the black community, because of oppression, racism and insensitivities around this, people have generally been suspicious of statutory bodies. For many the attitude is, 'Let's do it ourselves. Let's deal with this in-house.' The idea of having "white benchmarks" that you have to be seen to be reaching can be immensely off-putting.* (Hudson, a social worker of African-Caribbean/African-American heritage and an adoptive father, quoted in Massiah (2005, p 79))

The invasion of privacy is often quoted as a barrier but this is not a difficult problem to overcome, if applicants are helped to understand the reason for the assessment and why it may seem intrusive.

> *In many black communities there is a tradition of fostering and adopting in the extended family, but it's something you do as a favour and out of generosity. You don't expect to be vetted beforehand and it's sometimes felt to be quite insulting that you have this generous motive to take a child in, only to be asked questions about whether you are capable of it or whether you are the right person. That jars with people. A lot of black people can't get their heads round why they have to be scrutinised when they are doing something so selfless... I think an education task needs to be carried out in the black community about child protection issues.* (Nita, a 43-year-old adoptive parent of Anglo-Asian descent (quoted in Massiah, 2005, p 76))

There are other cultural barriers to consider when recruiting from black and minority ethnic families, such as the stigma around infertility issues. There could be a male/female divide, which makes it inappropriate to discuss certain issues together.

> *More training should be given to social workers about working with black families. Culturally we are different and this needs to be acknowledged.* (Black adopter)

There are many foster carers who are willing to continue looking after a child on a permanent basis without the legality of adoption, which may be alien to their culture. Some cultures do not accept children being born out of wedlock or the changing of names, and naming a child can have great significance. This is where Special Guardianship, an option now available in England and Wales following the Adoption and Children Act 2002, could be a useful alternative to adoption.

Valuing black and minority ethnic carers

Valuing black and minority ethnic prospective carers at all stages of the adoption process is crucial. This begins from when prospective carers make their first enquiry to an agency, through to the welcome they receive, the treatment they receive at preparation groups, including whether or not they feel sufficiently included in the home study/assessment process, to the recommendation or not for approval at the panel.

The adoption or permanence panel's understanding of the suitability of black and minority ethnic carers is crucial and all panels should reflect the community they serve. When applicants attend panel sessions, it is encouraging for them to see that minority groups are represented.

Sally Baffour is a black adoptive parent and sits on a number of adoption panels in London. She is the founder and co-ordinator of an organisation called Thank U, which holds fundraising dinners in aid of children's welfare in Africa and the Caribbean. These events provide an opportunity to promote adoption and fostering to black families and a number of local authorities in London have sponsored these events or advertised in the programme. At the time of writing, she was producing and hosting a 13-week television talk show called Adoption Matters on the Sky channel, Original Black Entertainment, for which she was also seeking sponsorship and advertising from local authorities seeking to reach prospective black adopters. She also advises black people, on an individual basis, about their applications and assessment.

Some of the difficulties in recruitment, she says, are due to problems of communication between social services and black communities.

I have spoken to adoption teams in many London boroughs and some have told me that the proportion of black and minority ethnic children they have waiting for adoption is as high as 70 or 80 per cent. The ads for black adopters that local authorities place in the mainstream media are seen by everyone but people are reluctant to come forward, and I believe this is due to the chequered history black people have had with social services.

A totally new approach is needed. People may have heard about others who have been turned down as prospective adopters for reasons which seem silly, and so they go into it with an element of trepidation. There are some questions that black families will perceive as trick questions. They should be giving straightforward answers, but instead they are sometimes guarded and find themselves being misunderstood by white social workers. It is not a question of being racist – the social workers just don't know how things work within our community, how family members support each other and so on. Social services departments need more black social workers in senior positions who can pick up things like this.

We need to educate both sides and recognise where the weaknesses are. For instance, if people have had some criminal activity in their past they would probably not divulge it, but – provided the crime was nothing to do with children – I would explain that it would not rule them out. I say: 'There is nothing wrong with telling social workers; it won't go against you if you can explain how long ago it happened, what the experience has done for you and why it might make you the best placed person to help these children now.' I help people to understand how to present themselves.

The black community needs to be educated about the way things are done in social services departments and why social workers ask the questions they do.

Professionals now need to work consistently and patiently to build bridges with these communities. Widening the pool of available black and minority ethnic families requires continuously building and maintaining good and positive relationships with minority ethnic communities.

Recruiting black and minority ethnic carers or adopters is, of course, only one stage of the process; retaining them is equally, if not more, critical. This is explored in the following chapters.

7 What works?

Agency planning, policies and practice

Policies and procedures need to be sensitive to black and minority ethnic communities and their needs. We must avoid creating stereotypes and making assumptions, while being aware of the discrimination and prejudice that minority ethnic communities face in this society. Does the agency have a policy regarding applicants who do not speak English? Are they welcomed in or automatically weeded out? Will preparation groups have a black perspective, and involve black and minority ethnic applicants in a way that is appropriate, culturally sensitive and relevant? How will you keep panel members informed of cultural, racial and religious matters?

Response

So interested people make enquiries – what next? Do your policies and procedures reflect how black and minority ethnic families need to be supported during and after the process? It is really good to have a clear policy about what the agency would be prepared to offer in order to secure the right family for a specific child. For instance, are you willing to look at re-housing if a family is prepared to take a sibling group? Would you consider a family whose spoken English is limited? These policy decisions need to be in place before the situation arises.

Is there recognition of the high number of families who live in deprived areas and the effects on housing, employment and transport, and are these factors acknowledged in the support packages that are offered to families? Many black and minority ethnic families may have incomes much below the national average – how will this be addressed and for what duration? Are you sensitively aware of cultural differences in the various black and minority ethnic communities, or is any black family deemed to be enough?

The assessment process is very time-consuming for both parties and the relationship between the assessor and prospective carers is paramount. How long things take is often a key concern for prospective enquirers. Maintaining the right approach can make a positive experience of the assessment and matching process. In the main, the assessment process is there for a purpose; however, people's apprehensions need to be addressed. Forward-planning each stage with applicants and going over what has already been done at each visit helps to allay some of these fears.

Recruitment strategies

Agencies need a recruitment strategy to ensure they can recruit the type of carers who are needed for the children who need them.

Goldstein *et al* (2000) states that the first requirement is for a pro-active, diligent and rolling recruitment programme for foster carers and adopters. This must be based on an audit of the children "in need" and children looked after in the local authority. Attention must be paid to recruiting a range of carers and adoptive parents who can provide a continuity of culture, language and religion.

Case studies

A large council in the south-east

The agency has a recruitment strategy working group which continually monitors the backgrounds of children requiring adoptive homes against the profiles of initial enquiries. In the main it is our experience that our agency does attract a wide spectrum of would-be adopters who broadly represent the ethnic mix within the county.

We are going to try and improve our branding so that we visually convey in all our recruitment literature the range of ethnic backgrounds that we seek adopters for. We are also planning to have a dedicated page on our new website for ethnic minority enquirers.

We have placed adverts in The Voice *and BHM (a Black History Month guide).*

Recently we held a focus group meeting with black adopters to discuss with them how we could appeal more to black and minority ethnic adopters. The focus group was a particularly useful initiative. We deliberately held this meeting away from social services offices and hired a comfortable room in a local hotel with good access.

The agency has learned lessons from the NCH (2004) research, which has informed our thinking about placements.

Kirklees Metropolitan Borough Council

Our recruitment strategy sets out how many black and minority ethnic families are needed, from which backgrounds and for what type of children, but also recognises that we will need to use interagency placements.

Recruitment of black and minority ethnic adopters is always on the agenda. We always state that we are particularly keen to recruit black and minority ethnic carers and include this message in all our advertising. We have two Asian workers who lead on this as well.

We have benefited from a strong group of Asian workers in the local adoption consortium who jointly run the adoption preparation training for Yorkshire agencies. As a result we are doing well with recruitment and approval of carers.

Involving communities by consulting them about recruitment, particularly from the start, helps to forge and build long-term relationships. It also enables the agency to challenge its own thinking or even long-standing beliefs. What do you want to know and what are the key questions when consulting minority ethnic communities? What would it be like to be in their shoes? A greater mutual understanding and awareness might result from an evaluation of your service and how the community perceives it.

Does your authority currently have a recruitment policy that has made specific reference to black and minority ethnic communities? If you have developed a recruitment strategy on how you will reach members of black and minority ethnic communities, did you involve members of the community? By involving communities in the design, delivery and evaluation of your services, you may get useful feedback. Use their suggestions on how you can get your messages across without causing offence or being patronising. By developing this kind of relationship with your local communities, you will be developing culturally sensitive policies and procedures which will bear results.

Remember that men and women may have different views and expectations – in some cultures there are particularly strong differences. It is also important to find out about how age groups are represented in a community and to consult a cross-section, as opinions may differ according to age.

Developing your recruitment strategy

Start by researching the image of your agency through local community groups and analyse any prevalent myths or perceptions. Work out the number of carers that you need against the number and characteristics of children waiting and publicise the ethnic profile of the families that you are looking for. Get a real understanding of the demographics of your authority and where communities go within your borough. Then consider targeted approaches, in or outside the borough, depending on the groups that you are trying to attract.

Recruitment strategies should be monitored and evaluated on a quarterly basis against outcome indicators or measures.

Checklist for developing a recruitment strategy

- Ascertain who the children waiting are. What are their needs? How many?

- Assess what type of carers you will need and how many.

- Identify what you will do or what methods you will use to recruit them.

- Ascertain your current and future staffing needs for effective recruitment.

- Be clear about your budget for recruitment.

- Be aware of what works and does not work, based on information from the previous recruitment campaign.

- Estimate what percentage of carers can reasonably be recruited locally and what percentage will have to be recruited from another given geographical area.

- Pinpoint areas where it is possible to develop long-term links.

- Designate one key person to be the link between the agency and the community – preferably someone who reflects the ethnicity of the largest proportion of the children waiting.

- Use existing carers and/or young people who have left care to take part in recruitment activities

So you have your recruitment strategy – what next? Do you need a plan of action? It would be a good idea to have a wall-planner to keep an eye on the tasks to be accomplished over the year. Allocate tasks with a back-up plan just in case of any unexpected circumstances.

Develop your agency's unique selling point

Each agency has particular strengths: some agencies have particularly good support structures, while others may offer financial incentives or pride themselves on the service they give at the initial point of contact. Knowing what you are really good at gives you the opportunity to add value to your service. These benefits should be highlighted in your recruitment material so that prospective carers can begin to buy in to what you have on offer.

Recruitment material

Personalising your service by devising recruitment packs specifically for black and minority ethnic heritage families has a resource implication but may be valuable in the long run. When designing new recruitment material, consider whether or not to translate it into other languages. If people have not had the opportunity to go to school and are therefore unable to read in their own language, what is the point of translating information into that language? It may be more effective to deliver the same message using pictures or verbally. Or how about using dual translation? This gives other family members who may have been educated and speak English an opportunity to read the information and translate appropriately. There may not even be the equivalent word in another language for words that describe a service, but other words could be used to explain it.

In recruitment material, it is useful to demonstrate your agency's inclusive approach by using language and images that reflect the looked after children population and therefore the types of carers you need for them. There is little point in having display advertising or posters in local community centres that show white children if, for example, there is a large number of black and minority ethnic children awaiting permanent placement. Equally, there is little point in having material showing a large number of black and minority ethnic children if your agency has no such children awaiting placement!

Remember to make your recruitment material available in ways in which it will be noticed by the people you want to target.

Consulting faith groups to find out how your message is viewed by members may give you an insight into what you need to address in future. The London borough of Tower Hamlets invited discussion with a local imam (spiritual head of the Islamic faith) and got valuable feedback that helped them to develop their current recruitment material.

A key worker for recruitment

Having a key worker with the responsibility for recruitment can free up valuable social worker time. This person could be employed to link with local ethnic communities. A great deal of their work will be outside office hours, but financial incentives could make the job attractive and it would be another way to develop word of mouth publicity in your area. Keeping close to communities may bring opportunities that are unexpected but could be fruitful.

The Fostering Network survey, *Improving Effectiveness in Foster Care Recruitment*, found that in 2005–2006 over half of the foster services questioned had a post dedicated to the recruitment of foster carers, and those that did have such a post were more successful in recruiting foster carers. Two-thirds of the dedicated posts were responsible for recruiting both foster carers and adoptive families.

The successful key worker also has an intangible quality – they usually believe that they can make a difference.

Outsourcing recruitment

Some London boroughs are contracting out some of their recruitment to specialists or consultancies with expertise in reaching black and minority ethnic communities. These people may have a wide range of contacts within particular communities and be able to tap into networks, events and media that your team may not be aware of. They may also have special expertise in marketing. This does cost money but it may allow you to compensate for gaps, for instance, if you have a team that is predominantly white or if your team does not include anyone with expertise in marketing and communications. Alternatively, you may want to contract out some recruitment work to people who have community development skills and/or links with particular communities.

Communication strategy

A communication strategy should provide a comprehensive basis for working with the press and other media and offer an opportunity to establish good links with a local journalist. For instance, BAAF works closely with a freelance journalist, Yinka Sunmonu, who writes for *The Voice*, a weekly newspaper for and about the black community. Every year Sunmonu writes at least two specialist articles for *The Voice* on adoption and fostering. She is knowledgeable about the subject and is able to cover stories as an expert because BAAF has had a working partnership with her over a number of years. She is fully aware of the issues and actively wants to make a difference to black and minority ethnic children's lives.

Building a relationship with a local journalist could prove very fruitful.

Communication tip

Try using audio, video or DVD as a means for communicating with communities. Communication strategies sometimes assume that people speak and read a single language; however, there could be a variation even within one family. For instance, you may have a family in which the mother speaks a Punjabi dialect which is not a written language but also speaks Urdu and can read some Urdu but is not confident enough to read or speak English. The father may be fluent in Punjabi and Urdu and reads Urdu but is not confident in reading English, although he speaks English reasonably well. Their two children, educated in this country, are fluent in both written and oral English.

Consulting communities

Your agency may be in an area where there are a relatively high number of people from black or other minority ethnic communities, in which case, methods of reaching them might be fairly straightforward. If you have a smaller number of people from these communities, you will probably need to work harder. Regardless of the ethnic profile of your area, it is good practice to consult and involve communities before devising recruitment campaigns.

The Census data for your UK country (there are different data for England and Wales, Northern Ireland and Scotland) are the best source for finding out about minority ethnic groups in your area. The Local Area Labour Force Survey statistics are also very useful, as are your local authority planning or economic development departments. Some information can be found in local journals and magazines, which have been produced by local organisations or local authorities. The Council for Race Equality (CRE) and local equality councils will also provide statistics, as well as surveys conducted by community organisations.

Many areas also now have "observatories" providing data and intelligence on a range of economic, social and environmental issues. These observatories maintain websites and databases of current research and can identify where particular minority ethnic communities are located, along with other useful information on age profiles, employment and so on (see www.regionalobservatories.org.uk).

It is important to find out more about the ethnicity, language, religion and culture of the communities in your area because it makes you aware of any particular needs that they might have when using your service. These factors may also affect how communities see themselves and others. There may be important distinctions, such as definition by religious affiliation, rather than ethnicity. You need to be aware of them if your strategy is to be successful.

Improving social workers' and panel members' awareness

What is the social workers' and panel members' understanding of cultural differences and variations in home and child-rearing values? Will training be provided? Some knowledge of the geographical area, of the history of specific communities, and the range of community-based amenities such as churches, mosques and community centres, is essential. You should seek advice on cultural and ethnic issues before approaching the community.

How to begin to develop your awareness of different communities

- Consider your attitudes and beliefs.

- Admit being unaware of certain elements and work towards becoming increasingly aware and sensitive to other people's ethnicity, culture, heritage, gender, class, socio-economic status, sexual orientation and religion.

- Acknowledge how your own ethnicity, culture, heritage, gender, class, socio-economic status, sexual orientation and religion have impacted upon your own history and experiences and which in turn have influenced you.

- Recognise the limits of your competence and expertise with regard to working with difference in terms of ethnicity, heritage, gender, class, socio-economic status, sexual orientation and religion.

- Demonstrate comfort, tolerance and sensitivity to difference that may exist between your own and other people's ethnicity, heritage, gender, class, socio-economic status, sexual orientation and religion.

- Recognise your knowledge level.

- Identify specific knowledge about your own ethnic background and how it has affected you personally and professionally.

- Demonstrate your knowledge and understanding of discrimination in any form and how it affects you personally and professionally.

- Recognise your own social impact on others, your communication style and that of other people. Consider how your style may inhibit or encourage and anticipate how this may impact on others.

Developing your skills

- Look for educational, consultative and training experiences to improve your understanding of and effectiveness in working with ethnicity, heritage, gender, class, socio-economic status, sexual orientation and religion.

- Constantly seek to understand yourself within your own multiple identities (such as: black, working class, female, Christian) and actively strive to unlearn the various behaviours and processes that covertly and overtly communicate and perpetrate oppression.

Working with faith groups

Most places of worship are fertile ground for recruitment: churches, mosques, temples, synagogues and gurdwaras can be found all over the UK. Congregations tend to represent a broad spectrum of their communities – unemployed people; different age ranges; semi-skilled, business and professional workers.

Many of these places of worship help to address local community issues and needs through faith-based networking. On an informal basis, faith groups provide valuable mutual support opportunities for young and older people as well as advice and support where needed. Faith groups can be a good starting point for reaching more enclosed communities.

Consider tailoring recruitment campaigns to align with particular faith groups. It is important to remember that not all faith groups will be interested in becoming active partners with agencies. However, if the communication channels are open, interest could change over time.

Another point to bear in mind is that the relationship between faith and ethnic identity can be close. For example, if two people from Asia and Africa share the same religion, their common faith might be more important to them than the fact that they come from different ethnic groups.

> *I do think there were some assumptions made as the process began. We are both of Asian origin and our culture is the same, was one assumption made. However, I come from a Bangladeshi background and my partner has an Asian-Caribbean background, so we have very different religious backgrounds.* (Prospective adopters)

Since the terrorist attacks on New York on 11 September 2001, there has been increased hostility towards the Muslim community and other minority ethnic communities, which has raised tensions within the individual faith communities. There is currently a debate on whether religion is an identity which requires recognition and protection within a global but diverse society.

Checklist for working with faith groups

- Remember that each faith community is not a homogeneous group and there are cultural, ethnic and also religious differences between people of the same faith.

- Challenge religious stereotypes, particularly in media reporting.

- Find out what is good practice in working with faith communities.

- Train staff to be culturally and religiously sensitive.

- Use any information that your local authority has collected on faith communities to enable it to gauge the proportional take-up of services.

- Be aware of the faith demographics in your area, the local faith community centres and places of worship.

- Start a database that includes the names of the leaders of different faiths; this could include the name of priests, pastors, bishops, reverends, elders, imams and rabbis.

- Create a yearly wall planner to identify important community events and religious festivals.

Recruitment methods

Word of mouth

Word of mouth is the best recommendation for any organisation. Agencies like Barnardo's Jigsaw and NCH Black Families report that many of their enquiries come from people who have heard other people tell of their good experiences. Using existing foster carers and adopters in recruitment campaigns is therefore most important. PACT (Parents and Children Together) gets its foster carers and adopters involved in recruitment events; for example, they help out at recruitment events held at their local supermarket or church. They hand out leaflets and talk to interested shoppers. How about using extended foster and adoptive family members and friends to help spread the message to their own communities or in training workshops or preparation sessions?

Key people

Social workers are a scarce resource and may not always be the best people to lead a recruitment drive. So how else can we build close relationships with minority ethnic groups? Perhaps a community worker or volunteers from the black community could take responsibility for recruitment activities. This post could have incentives in line with the number of carers who go on beyond the information stage; it could possibly be a part-time job, working specifically at weekends, in order to meet the most people.

Using key people consistently throughout is a great formula for gaining community trust. The St Francis Children's Society–Anancy Black Families Initiative use community co-ordinators: the community co-ordinator worker works part-time, and their duties are mainly developing links with minority ethnic communities with the aim of raising awareness of adoption. Also, involving young people who have been looked after in your campaigns can be a very

powerful message. Local representatives who have ethnic, religious and business connections are especially good at helping to get the community to engage with the issues.

Focus groups

Hold focus groups, invite the members to identify any communication barriers or just to evaluate what is currently being done. Focus groups are one of a range of low-cost methods for rapidly collecting information, gaining ideas and assisting decision-making.

Working with the media

Media, including local media, that are directed to certain black and minority ethnic groups are referred to here as specialist media. We must all be aware that the media help to frame the perceptions of people both positively and negatively. Therefore, developing a good relationship with the media can help dispel myths about adoption and fostering and project clear, responsible messages to the whole community about the need for more carers.

A specialist medium, like Kismet Radio or Choice FM, offers an opportunity for agencies to communicate with families who may be uninterested in mainstream media. Portraying black people in a positive light is a necessary task for the specialist media because in the tabloid press black people are often portrayed quite negatively. Specialist media can bring the message home to a specific community. Using experiences from an existing adopter or foster carer and, for instance, using their own words in an editorial, can be very rewarding not only for the agency but for the carer or adopter as well. People like to be validated.

The media landscape for ethnic groups is fragmented, with family members accessing a wide range of different media in different places and at different times. This multiple consumption poses a difficulty when deciding which medium would be most effective for getting a message across. But there may be opportunities for creative niche marketing through specialist media that could hook into the specific ethnic and cultural interest of particular groups.

It is good to keep in touch with the specialist media's target audience: for instance, *Eastern Eye* newspaper is aimed at the second and third generation of British Asians. It has a weekly readership of around 20,000.

Although people of Indian origin under 40 probably consider mainstream media as more important than specialist media, some young women do enjoy watching Asian dramas with their mothers. The older generation, particularly Indian women, usually prefer Asian TV and radio programmes, whilst religious radio programmes are of particular importance to older people from the Pakistani and Bangladeshi communities.

The marked differences between the lifestyles of men and women, chiefly around paid work, child care and housework, could also have some impact on their opportunities and preferences for media consumption.

Younger women from Asian backgrounds between the ages of 25 and 45 who have recently arrived in the UK are keen to learn English and get involved in mainstream society, while older women tend to believe it may be "too late" for them. The older generation do not generally see themselves as British even if they have lived in the UK for a number of years.

Mainstream media should be used as well as specialist media in order to ensure that the various black and minority ethnic communities get the messages the agency wants to convey.

However, when profiling children to communities, be mindful of the messages you give to the community. As recently as January 2006, one child's profile referred to the shade of a child's skin tone when looking for a black heritage family. Why? The shade of a child's skin tone should not be a factor when finding the most appropriate family.

People from minority ethnic groups will engage with the messages if the messages are respectful. As mentioned earlier, it has been noted by Phillips (2000) that 87 per cent of local authorities have adopted a "colour-blind" approach to the needs of black children who are disabled. Here is an opportunity for an agency to address this issue by highlighting that this child is vulnerable to racism and discrimination on the basis of their ethnicity, as well as their disability.

Top tips for working with the media

- Build up a database of your local ethnic community publications and broadcast media.

- Develop a good working relationship with local journalists based on openness, honesty and trust.

- Agree the key messages and stick to them.

- Have a long-term strategy for featuring news stories that educate and inform communities about adoption and fostering and help to dispel myths and prejudices.

- Review your target media with the help of information from the Census or other sources. Always try to speak to editors of local papers to see if they would be willing to run joint campaigns, particularly during National Adoption Week and Fostering Fortnight.

- Think like a journalist – would this story be of interest to a particular audience? Always ask: 'What's the human interest in this story?'

- Do not assume that journalists will be well versed in fostering and adoption. Offer each journalist a fact sheet and updates to keep them informed.

- The media are in the business of reporting news stories, so do not expect them to ignore a story that they feel is newsworthy even if you do not agree.

- Scour your community and local press to keep up to date with what is happening and have leaflets ready to hand out at events.

Using the internet and your website

Raising awareness via the internet is an essential tool for communicating with black and minority ethnic communities, as indeed with the white communities, on a 24-hours a day basis. Internet sites such as Black Britain (www.blackbritain.co.uk), which provides daily news and information to black and minority ethnic communities, can be used for giving "drip-drip" messages to the community. Some agencies advertise their details, or even feature children's profiles, on such websites.

The BAAF website has developed specific pages for black and minority ethnic communities and includes information about the recruitment process and the characteristics of the children who are waiting to be adopted or fostered. The website has a facility for requesting more information, which is then sent to them by post. Any contact details received are used to follow up enquirers. The BAAF web pages also have links to individual agencies in London so that enquirers can access local information. In 2007, *Be My Parent* will also extend its service to a web-based family-finding service.

Your website is another way of engaging with your local minority ethnic communities. Could there be specific pages that reflect the benefits for families that come forward for black, Asian and mixed-heritage children? It would be helpful to have a system for tracking and following up email enquiries and for gathering information about the enquirers' ethnicity. Some agencies feature children's profiles on their website, where they have permission to do this.

Linking your site to other websites is another way to make the most of the Internet. Consider using websites such as Black Britain, Black UK Online, Red Hot Curry or Premier online (website addresses are listed under Useful Organisations).

Viral marketing is the new medium that has been developed to attract more enquiries using an alternative marketing approach. Word of mouth marketing is by no means a complete panacea to the recruiting of black heritage carers but it is an essential aspect. On-line viral marketing is the internet equivalent to word of mouth. More and more companies are using this method to raise awareness and generate interest. More about this type of marketing can be found in *Connected Marketing: The viral, buzz and word of mouth revolution* (edited by J Kirby and P Marsden, 2005, Butterworth-Heinemann).

Events and talks

Attending local and national events, if only to give out leaflets, is another way to engage with communities, but first get to know more about ethnic and religious festivals and traditions celebrated in your area.

Black History Month is celebrated in October. It tends to be a notable occasion that is talked about in schools and most local authorities organise events to commemorate the history of black people in their boroughs. Try to take advantage of events in your area, as they are a good way of connecting with a diverse community.

Use events and festivals such as the Brick Lane Festival and Notting Hill Carnival (both in London), *melas* and carnivals in other cities, Diwali and Chinese New Year celebrations, which offer good opportunities for handing out literature.

Scotland's biggest multicultural festival, the Mela in Edinburgh, is held every year in September. This provides a great opportunity to use a stall to target a range of prospective carers, particularly those from a South Asian background. Glasgow also holds a Mela.

Giving talks to cultural and religious groups is a great way to interact with the community. You do have to be mindful of the language you use. We are so used to slipping into social work jargon that we forget that the average person on the street would not recognise the terminology. With this in mind, these presentations give the enquirers who are keen and interested an opportunity to understand the kinds of children waiting for families. Introducing the process and procedures, the role of the panel, the matching stage and allowances, and the support available can help to alleviate concerns. Inviting an existing black foster carer or adopter to these meetings will bring home the reality of being a carer.

After attending events, have a follow-up procedure in place. Remember that people stay in touch using in a variety of different ways such as text, photo messaging, email, telephone and letter.

> *As a consortium, we sometimes do joint publicity, marketing and recruitment events – for instance, during National Adoption Week we will pay to hire a bus. We have also been to exhibitions: we had a stand at "Aspirations", an exhibition at Olympia for black professional people and this year we are going to an exhibition called "Voice of Nigeria".* (North London Adoption Consortium)

An increasing number of agencies now hold adoption exchange days. Prospective adopters from the local community are invited to attend and are given information about the children needing permanent placements. At some, information about specific children waiting is also available as printed material and sometimes, increasingly, conveyed through a short film that features the child. Ensure that black and minority ethnic applicants who have made enquiries and have put forward applications to adopt are invited, and feel included. Having black and minority ethnic agency staff as well as established carers to talk to will help, as will having a wide variety of refreshments, which will indicate that your agency has taken that extra step to cater to the needs of the diverse community that it serves.

National Adoption Week and Foster Care Fortnight

National Adoption Week is BAAF's annual campaign to raise awareness about adoption and to recruit more adoptive families. As part of this campaign, BAAF works with the national and the specialist media, including placing features in *The Voice*, *Caribbean Times* and *Asian Times*. BAAF staff and other agencies are also involved in interviews on

GMTV and local black and minority ethnic radio stations throughout the UK, highlighting the need for more black and minority ethnic families to come forward. Black, Asian and mixed-heritage children are featured on GMTV and in *The Voice*, and sometimes also in mainstream media.

Harvey Gallagher, BAAF's Marketing Director, says:

When we are developing the messages of the campaign, one of the key messages every year is the need for black and minority ethnic families. We make sure we reflect this in the wording and the images we use, as well as using BAAF spokespeople of different ethnicities. On GMTV we might present a vignette of a black child, an interview with a black person who has been adopted, and a professional working with black families.

Nimmy March, the actress, is a black woman who was adopted and she is a patron of BAAF. We ask Nimmy to act as a spokesperson for BAAF, particularly at times when she is in the public eye.

After each National Adoption Week, we monitor the immediate levels of interest and the number of enquiries that come about as a result of items in different media, and two to three years later we go back to all the enquirers to see whether any of them have gone on to become adopters.

When we featured children who needed adoptive families in The Sun, *we found that it was an effective way of reaching black and minority ethnic people, because of its huge circulation. Much smaller numbers read the minority ethnic press and the geographical spread tends to be more limited. But coverage in the ethnic media gives an important message – that we value what BME families can offer children.*

However, there is a limit to the level of detail and complexity that can be communicated via print media. Part of the challenge of the media message is getting the right balance – we don't want to generate thousands of enquiries from people who don't meet the needs of children waiting the longest. Generating too many enquiries just clogs up the system. What we really want is fewer but appropriate enquiries, from the people we need.

Your agency can capitalise on the national publicity generated by National Adoption Week, held in early November each year, by putting on your own recruitment events and contacting your local media.

Black and minority ethnic people who have recently seen articles in the national press or on national television about the need for families for children from these backgrounds may be more receptive to your message. Every year, the National Adoption Week team at BAAF give agencies a PR pack which advises them on how to involve the local media and providing case studies of other agencies which have done this successfully.

Foster Care Fortnight is a similar event held in May and organised by The Fostering Network. The Fostering Network and fostering services secure extensive media coverage during Foster Care Fortnight – in 2006 there were features on *The New Paul O'Grady Show* and GMTV, supplements in *The Mirror* and *The Independent* and articles in *The People* and the *Sunday Express* magazine, plus many items in the local press and on local radio.

Although newspapers and television programmes aimed at mass market audiences do not specifically target black and minority ethnic communities, there is no doubt that simply because of the huge numbers of viewers or readers they have, they can be effective in terms of reaching every section of the community.

Advertising

Advertising should be considered as a tool for raising interest in adoption or fostering and not for getting an immediate response. It is not the same as advertising a washing machine! It is preferable for enquirers to have thought through some of the implications and benefits of fostering or adoption and how it will impact on their lives. Most people who respond have been thinking about it for some time. Thus advertising is good for the "drip-drip" approach.

If you want to become more cost-effective at using advertising, then take a long hard look at your area and see what advertising opportunities there are. Some authorities have unlimited advertising opportunities within their own boroughs; putting messages on lamp-posts is one cost-effective method. Advertising campaigns in local and regional media including press and radio are also important and not necessarily expensive.

If you intend to use specialist media such as your local or ethnic press, then try to get an editorial or "advertorial" at the same time. It is good value for money if you can negotiate a feature on adoption and fostering at the same time as buying advertising space, and many magazines will be receptive to this idea.

A number of London agencies have used the *Metro* free newspaper to advertise, with varying degrees of success. Some received a very high response rate, whereas another agency reported that they did not get a single enquiry. Placing an advertisement is quite costly, but the paper does reach a wide audience.

Checklist for advertising

- Stop advertising if it is not working. People run advertising campaigns because they feel they ought to. If you are not really sure if a campaign is working, find a way to evaluate results and change the plan if necessary.

- Evaluating by testing and measuring outcomes from advertising is essential. Knowing how many people responded and how many were approved as carers can be used as a measurement tool against actual advertising costs.

- Remember that your headline/strap line is the most important part of your advertisement.

- In your advertising, as well as using images of black and minority ethnic children, make sure you get across the message that it is black and minority ethnic adoptive families that these children need.

- Attention, Interest, Desire and Action (AIDA) is the classic advertising format to follow in every advertisement.

- Remember that there are other ways of advertising than by using paid advertisements. Direct mail, word of mouth and strategic alliances may prove to be better, particularly for building relationships.

Ongoing campaigns

Ongoing campaigns are much better than one-off campaigns but the cost of advertising can be quite high. However, there are alternative methods of having an ongoing campaign that are cost-effective. Most local authorities have ways of creating cheap publicity. Many councils have free publications that carry advertisements and perhaps leaflets could be sent out with them or even with the council tax notices. Consider placing smaller advertisements on a regular basis, rather than one large advertisement on only one occasion. This way, readers will be reminded of your message over a particular period, rather than be told it only once.

Making links

How can other council services such as health, education, regeneration programmes or community centres be used to cascade your message? Is there a way of joint working or using other organisations' publications to get across your message? These are all strategies to consider when resources are scarce.

Try to take advantage of or partner existing services and initiatives that may be aimed at the community. For instance, school newsletters – could you contribute a good news story about an existing black adopter's or foster carer's experience? Local councils' neighbourhood renewal departments or community cohesion units will also be trying to forge links with the community – are there ways for you both to benefit by joining resources?

Get out into the community

Hairdressers, barbers and nail salons are great places for reading! So see if you can leave some leaflets around for people to pick up. The London Borough of Ealing did a consultation in the community that used their hairdressing salons and barbers as a focal point for their soundings.

Asian and African-Caribbean food shops could also be good places for putting up notices or posters about fostering and adoption. Speak to the owner of the premises and let them know why it is important for their customers to read about the black children waiting for families. It helps with building relationships, so they too can pass on your message.

Think outside the box

Have you tried getting your message across using alternative ways? How about promotional gifts such as bookmarks or keyrings or mugs as a giveaway item in libraries? Trying to think outside the box is sometimes very difficult to do on your own; getting a group of people together to call out ideas from the really stupid to the bizarre can produce just the right brilliant idea in between. And a novel approach could become a local talking point.

8 Recruitment with a new look

A different approach

Existing methods for recruiting black foster carers and black adopters should be reviewed. We need to take a more holistic approach. This chapter outlines some innovative ways in which we can engage communities as a part of a much broader spectrum of care for looked after black and minority ethnic children. It also suggests some ways in which agencies can ensure that they are sensitive and responsive to the needs of black and minority ethnic applicants.

What we should be trying to do is to tell people how they can make a difference to a black child in their area by becoming a mentor, independent visitor or child advocate, as well as highlighting the merits of kinship care, short break foster care, fostering and adoption. Communities should understand that a continuum of support is needed for some families and their children.

Whilst it is recognised that there are a number of minority workers within the public sector, there still need to be more black, Asian and mixed-heritage employees in managerial positions. For cultural changes to occur from the top down, black managers can play their part in contributing to best practice and at the same time improve services to BME communities.

If agencies were to amalgamate their recruitment for fostering and adoption, it would save the department money, children's services departments could give an inclusive message about the long-term care needs of looked after children, and potential carers could choose how to commit themselves. If they decide to foster, they may still go on to adopt at a later stage. Would this be such a bad thing? If it produces a constant stream of black and minority ethnic carers, then surely this would be beneficial.

How creative is our thinking and how prompt are the responses of our recruitment services towards inquiries from black and minority ethnic carers? If someone does not meet our criteria to adopt, do we lose that person or do we try to engage him or her in another way to support black, Asian and mixed-heritage children?

I saw in our paper about all those children needing families and I really did want to help. I wasn't thinking of adopting but I did think I could foster. Then when the social worker came and explained about it, I knew I wouldn't be able to manage. But then they said have you ever thought of being a part-time carer? There are children needing breaks from their foster carers or their own families. I hadn't heard about this before but I went to a meeting and then I got assessed and now I have this little black boy every other weekend. He's disabled and lives with a white foster family and his mum is in hospital. He likes it here because he knows I am the same as his family. (Black African-Caribbean short-break foster carer)

It is important for us to think of creative ways in which we can help people to feel positive and motivated enough not to give up. For instance, some black applicants may have anxieties about a criminal record check because they have experienced discrimination at the hands of the police. It will be important that any information received via criminal record checks is clarified, if necessary by consulting with other relevant agencies, and then very fully discussed with the applicants, to achieve an understanding of the context in which it arose, and a basis on which it can be fairly evaluated. By consistently offering a sensitive service, being absolutely open and honest, and above all by being supportive, we should begin to see more people completing the process.

It is also essential that any issue concerning the significance of criminal records information is resolved clearly at the stage when applicants are being assessed, otherwise the same queries may be raised again by matching panels.

Even if enquirers withdraw or are not approved, at least we will have left them with positive messages about how we treat black people. The impression that we make on those families making enquiries will permeate through to others in their network and outwards to the wider community. Dealing with initial enquiries promptly and respectfully is central to successful recruitment.

We then approached a voluntary agency and they were excellent. What made it good was the fact that we had a very experienced black adopter/social worker and a very experienced social worker who was white, facilitating the training. We were nervous about the training but the down-to-earth style of the facilitators made it enjoyable for us. (A black adopter)

If possible, offer to hand-deliver initial reading material to give you an early opportunity to find out whether interpreters might be needed, allay any fears or misconceptions and to talk about adoption in more detail if asked. Each enquiry then needs to be monitored with a follow-up call of encouragement. What matters in recruitment is perseverance rather than quick results.

There is no magic formula for recruiting black and minority ethnic families but the agencies that have been successful in recruiting them have a similar approach, which often depends on one or two members of staff who are passionate about finding the right placement for black children. These workers play an active role in participating in local events, they make it their business to get to know their area, they get involved with communities and they never give up. Their motivation, their skill and commitment are innate and are not easily transferable. They follow through from the initial enquiry to assessment and on to approval; they do not lose contact with the people they have recruited, even long after the children have been placed.

This kind of relationship builds trust and from trust comes the key to recruiting by word of mouth. People buy into other people's experiences and the way they are treated.

The agency I approached was very quick in getting to know me more when I made the very first phone call. I didn't really know that much about adoption. I had rung the fostering team first because I wanted to look after a child on a long-term basis and they said I should contact the adoption team. So I did. The person that I spoke to wanted to come around as soon as possible to tell me more about how the adoption process works. It certainly was not what I expected. Also, I can't remember now exactly whether or not she was the person I spoke to on the phone or not, but the person who came around to deliver the information was just as nice. All this in a week – that's what I call service. (A black adopter)

Alan Rushton (2003) recommends that the nature of the initial contact with the agency should be explored to discover which factors are associated with follow-through (for example, warmth of reception, time to talk, experienced receptionist and appropriate amount of information). The report also stresses that research into the cultural competence of agencies in their recruitment, assessment, preparation and support activities would be of considerable benefit, and that there is a need to investigate which models are better received by different groups.

None of us, no matter how culturally aware we may be, will know everything. There is always an aspect to learn more about, whether it is to do with religion, heritage, culture or family customs.

We were dreading the home visits but our social worker put us at ease and was very friendly and had very good communication skills. Although she was not very familiar with all of the cultural and religious aspects of our lifestyle, she was very open about her ignorance and willing to learn. She did not patronise and did not make assumptions. (Asian adoptive father)

One way of raising interest is to ask existing black and minority ethnic foster carers and their extended support networks, as well as existing adopters, to help. They could perhaps act as mentors for prospective carers undergoing assessment. How about holding an annual event where old hands and new could meet and mingle?

A number of prospective black and minority ethnic adopters have said they would benefit from joining a support group while being assessed – who better to run it than experienced black carers? Having a good relationship with black foster carers and adopters enables agencies to hear their views, whether positive or negative, about the service they are getting, and it enables carers to offer ideas for recruitment.

Money is important for people with low incomes. How about a one-off payment when a family has been approved, or giving a gift voucher for introducing someone to the agency? We should always be clear about grants, benefits and allowances from the start. But we also have to be careful not to give the wrong impression.

I was told a certain figure regarding the settling-in grant and then I wasn't offered that figure at all. In the end I went through their complaints procedure and at Stage 2 they found in my favour. (A black adopter)

Childminders, another group of people who already have experience of looking after other people's children, might also help to recruit adopters or even consider providing more permanent care themselves.

An area of concern for professionals has been family-finding for children whose parents have mental health problems. The average person does not understand how mental illness may or may not affect the child now or at a later stage, and what kind of support there would be in place from the agency if the child presents with difficulties later on. Consultation with communities about their views on mental health may lead to a new perspective for preparation groups, as different cultures/communities may well view mental health quite differently.

Similarly, the recruiting for the black disabled child should focus on the child's needs, rather than the labels to describe him or her. When we begin to demystify the umbrella terms that are used for mental health and disability, we may then begin to find families who would be willing to care for a child with special needs.

If we learn to focus on solutions, then most people can develop an understanding of how they might cope in any given situation. Why not invite someone from the medical profession to take an active role when information evenings are held or during the assessment? Putting potential carers in touch with the specialist agencies such as SCOPE (the organisation for raising awareness about cerebral palsy) or MIND (for mental health) could help them to access or manage provision or support on offer in the future. You could also invite either of these groups to take part in preparation group meetings.

Sharing examples of positive stories will always have a strong influence. Black people are very keen to hear from black carers who have coped, or are coping, with children who have a mental health history or disability. Face-to-face is best but not always possible. Perhaps a video recording of a black carer or the voices of black children who have grown up in care talking about their experiences would be equally well received. Maybe this video could cover how different cultures or communities approach mental health or disability.

In view of the particular difficulties in recruiting black adopters for older black boys, we could consider other long-term placements to meet their needs. Because black boys tend to wait far longer than any others in the care system, new packages are needed that will act as an incentive for long-term carers to come forward. These packages do not have to be based solely on money; they could also include the kind of support that would be made available if, for instance, the child is excluded from school.

The myths around black boys are ultimately rooted in a discriminatory culture of low expectations and a societal failure to convey self-belief and hope to black boys, and need to be challenged by innovative practice. There are a number of organisations operating in the London area that mentor black boys (see useful organisations in *Resources*). Such organisations could be approached to link in with black carers and to provide good role models for older black boys. A very flexible approach is required for children for whom it will be difficult to find families, if they are not to find themselves left to "make do" in placements which – in the short or longer term – will further damage them.

Assessment and preparation

The way we prepare and support black carers will have a direct impact on the success of further recruitment.

How we talk with people from minority ethnic communities is crucial and this is where the attitudes of workers are so important. Body language, intonation and establishing rapport with someone are absolutely critical. We all bring some element of ourselves into that first interaction, assessment process or final judgment about whether the application should be taken any further or whether the applicant should be approved and we need to have a good knowledge of ourselves, regardless of ethnicity, culture, or religion.

Until we have a true understanding of our own prejudices, preferences, class, dislikes, likes, values, beliefs and also societal factors that lie within us, how can we truly reflect upon another's person's life experiences, view of the world and family background, and make good sense of these? It is this understanding of diversity that is essential. Just because we subscribe to the same school of thought or we have been socialised in the same way does not mean that we have a true understanding of each other's personal experience or the stance we take in order to survive.

Training and awareness in these areas should be frequently reviewed to ensure best practice not only by agency staff, but also for panel members and senior management. Explaining to applicants at the very beginning why assessment and preparation may feel intrusive can help to dispel any anxiety later.

During the assessment process the social worker should not make assumptions. The prospective black family's values and beliefs should be reviewed alongside the social worker's own beliefs and values before he or she makes judgments. If the applicants break appointments, for instance, it need not imply a lack of motivation on their part. For example, if the agency and the applicants do not share the same approach to strict time-keeping and adhering to plans, this is something to discuss fully at an early stage, and a realistic compromise reached that works for all sides. For example, looked after children will often need support in keeping appointments with many professionals and in maintaining contact visits (and telephone availability) with their family, and this requires good time managements and personal organisation from carers. We may be dealing with issues that have not been a priority in their culture or their lives previously but which they will have to confront or revisit as part of the adoptive parent or foster carer task.

Giving feedback regularly during the assessment period means that there will be no surprises to cause ill feelings later. Issues around ethnicity, identity and discrimination should be discussed separately and together in mixed partnerships. Exploring elements such as internalised indoctrination can be useful as part of the assessment process.

> *I think the main thing we experienced as a mixed-race couple is that all social workers and panel members directed questions of ethnicity at me and asked me how as a white woman I will be able to care for a mixed-race child: no-one ever asked my partner how he feels or what his thoughts and feelings are about a mixed-race child, as if he should know because he's black, and that the children will look more like him than me. This is regardless of the fact that he hasn't raised a mixed-race child in a mixed relationship and we will seek to face challenges together.* (Mixed-heritage adopters)

All prospective adopters, black or white, need to be fully trained, assessed and prepared to meet the needs of the specific child to be placed with them, including the need to keep the child connected to his or her birth family. Massiah (2005) comments that black adopters should be prepared for the possibility of living with a traumatised child. They should consider the impact the child will have on their own family and the impact they will have on the child.

> *The matching process was a real eye opener! We were astonished how one local authority had matched a child with us, which was quite inappropriate. We could have quite easily gone through and adopted the child as the authority was trying to push us to, but we had to take a stance and say no. The inappropriate matching was due to a lot of cultural assumptions being made and the needs of the birth mum were being placed above the long-term needs of the child. It was scary.* (Asian adopters)

When running adoption preparation groups, trainers need to be sensitive to the composition of the group, paying particular attention to how they will include and address the need of group members who are from minority ethnic groups, especially if they are on their own amongst a large white group; the same would apply to single applicants and how they might feel in a group otherwise entirely made up of couples. It would be important to make clear that differences will be respected and that any discriminatory comments from anyone in the group should be challenged.

You might hold separate preparation groups for black and minority ethnic applicants. Barnardo's New Families in Shipley, Bradford have set up an Asian Adopters Preparation Group. It gives the opportunity for prospective adopters and foster carers to attend preparation groups that are run using Urdu and Punjabi languages. You may be able to run these jointly with other agencies in the local area, offering each other places when space allows.

Be aware, when providing course material, that some people may be unable to read English well and may need to have it translated. You may need to arrange for interpreters if you know there will be participants who do not speak English. Good preparation must lead to good matching and continuing support.

Support

In terms of support, there is not a lot of it. I must say, it has been very much about finding out what we need to do for our daughter. This includes issues like obtaining a passport, child benefit, etc. I would say that my overall impression is that social workers are so busy that as soon as a child is placed and the reviews show that the child is bonding, they divert all their attention to children within the system. I would appreciate it if agencies provided more in terms of support after a child has been placed just as much (if not even more) as when the initial training was done. The key here is that a child has a whole lifetime to live with parents and all the support and information that adoptive parents can get would go a long way to help society. (Black adopters)

Supporting black adopters is crucial and the support on offer must be spelled out during recruitment. In England and Wales, adoption support is now a statutory requirement and the adoption support plan must include an assessment of needs for the child, the adopters and the birth family. In Scotland, adoption support is also a duty and this will be strengthened by new legislation, when the Adoption and Children (Scotland) Bill (introduced in March 2006) comes into force as expected in 2008. Limited adoption support is available in Northern Ireland; the system is currently being reviewed.

Adopters have to know exactly what the plan covers and how long they will receive support. Black carers often ask why support for foster children diminishes when they are adopted, because the children have the same needs regardless of the type of placement.

Means-tested financial support more in line with foster care allowances can now be given to adopters, but individual agencies will devise their own guidelines. It may have to be accepted that many black carers will need financial support in order to adopt. One could ask, can we make more secure placements by offering generous adoption support from the very beginning, rather than grudgingly or at crisis point when the placement threatens to disrupt? We need to become more proactive and engage with approved adopters so that we can learn lessons and change practice to suit the need.

Agencies could begin to look at a more inclusive approach to supporting adoptive families apart from individual adoption support plans. While annual events such as summer picnics and winter parties are great, how about running regular workshops on topics chosen by adopters and how about a group for adoptive fathers? Men do not always get catered for in this way, as they are not normally seen as the main carer. If they are the main carer, a group would be a good way to learn from each other and share experiences. Or how about a telephone support link run by other black adopters?

Support groups

Some adoption support organisations offer counselling and support groups. Since May 2005, the BAAF-ALG project for recruiting minority ethnic adopters runs a support group for black adopters.

I find the group very supportive as I feel safe being around others that have decided to adopt. It's not easy and we share the struggles together, giving each other advice on the whole process, its ups and downs. There is something about strength in numbers – I don't feel isolated. Moreover, I believe that adoption is still a taboo subject but even more so amongst black people and when I joined the group I immediately felt: 'They're like me – what a relief!' I see this group as a lifeline. (Black adopter)

BAAF has had many requests to facilitate a support group for black adopters who are going through the process. Finding families is just the first step in the process of recruiting. The next vital step is holding on to them. A vast number of people drop out after making an initial enquiry and this may be due to a number of reasons. They may self-select themselves out; they may find the process too intrusive and too long; or their circumstances may have changed. There may be a need for mentors of some kind who can be advocates for the process itself. These mentors could assist with training and provide support to prospective carers or adopters, in a way that will not compromise the assessment, and could be an important factor in not losing people after their initial enquiry. For some people it may be a journey on which some extra company would really go a long way.

Teenage support groups particularly aimed at children who are black and fostered or adopted should be encouraged from secondary transfer stage.

There are also support groups for people who have adopted a child from another country. NCH Black Families runs a support group for adoptive fathers. Feedback so far has been very positive because their needs are different to those of adoptive mothers.

Single adopters

Agencies are increasingly accepting of single people as adopters. The Government does not collect figures on the number of single adopters and foster carers.

Single people can be conscious of being in the minority in adoption preparation groups and trainers need to be sensitive to this.

Single adopters often feel isolated regardless of their support network, and a specific support group to address their particular needs might be welcomed. The support group could take off on its own once it is set up. Most single adopters just want to be able to share their experiences with others who know how it feels to be a lone parent of an adopted child. And what about setting up a baby-sitting service for single black adopters?

> *It would have been nice to have someone to talk to who was going through the same process.*
> (Single adopter quoted in Massiah, 2005)

An increasing number of single black and minority ethnic women are coming forward to adopt. A single-parent family can be an important resource and must be welcomed. Interestingly, in a compilation of the experiences of black adopters titled *Looking After our Own: The stories of black and Asian adopters* (Massiah, 2005), the majority of contributors were single adoptive parents. Not all of them had received the welcome that they deserved: nevertheless, all of them had persevered and had gone on to adopt. We do hear of numbers of single applicants waiting for a child to be placed with them. This is a disheartening experience for the single applicants themselves, and can send out a negative message for others who may be considering coming forwards. Single adopters are as valuable a resource as any other, and must be given equal consideration.

A Good Practice Guide titled *Recruiting, Assessing and Supporting Single Carers and Adopters*, by Bridget Betts (forthcoming), offers valuable guidance for social workers, and the recommendations made in that guide can usefully be adapted and

incorporated into the general guidance offered here. This guide will be available from BAAF in 2007.

Lesbian and gay adopters

Following the implementation of the Adoption and Children Act 2002 in England and Wales, lesbian and gay adopters can now apply to adopt jointly, as can any other unmarried couple. In Scotland, a similar change is proposed and, if passed, is expected to come into force in 2008. Same-sex couples are already assessed and approved together, although only one of them can adopt. Northern Ireland is currently (2006) considering this as part of its adoption review.

Like single adopters, same-sex couples can provide a secure, safe and loving family. Many lesbians and gay men, singly as well as in partnerships, have successfully fostered or adopted children. In some cases, it has been clear that for some children, being placed in a household headed by women, is the desired placement. As we have said elsewhere in this guide, black and minority ethnic lesbians and gay men could also be targeted in recruitment campaigns, for example, using the gay press, and should be made as welcome as any other applicant. Assessing the capabilities of lesbians and gay men to offer family life for waiting children needs a greater awareness of a number of factors that will be particular to their situation, family environment, networks, partnership arrangements and lifestyles. And remember, that just as in other partnerships, lesbians and gay men can also be in mixed-race partnerships. A Good Practice Guide titled *Recruiting, Assessing and Supporting Lesbian and Gay Carers and Adopters*, by Gerald Mallon and Bridget Betts (2005), offers valuable guidance for social workers, and the recommendations made in that guide can usefully be adapted and incorporated into the general guidance offered here.

Disabled adopters

The underlying prejudice against disabled people operates, inevitably, throughout the adoption process. Society broadly does not even accept that disabled people should conceive and rear their own biological children, let alone become adopters of someone else's child.

Prejudice begins with the agency's recruitment stage: how many posters or leaflets positively welcome disabled people as carers, valuing the resilience which they might bring? Even if approved, we know from repeated anecdotes that disabled adults have especial difficulty in being matched with a child. Semi-plausible excuses are often used to justify why a particular match should not be made with an approved disabled adopter, and issues exhaustively explored during the assessment are rehearsed again: supports, housing, capability and so on.

There is also an unspoken view that disabled adults should be matched with disabled children, regardless of the objectively assessed needs of the child or capacities of the adult. Disabled adults may indeed feel that what they have learned from their particular experience of adversity could be usefully applied on behalf of a child with an impairment. However, there is no reason why they should not be considered for the full range of children; indeed the resourcefulness and determination which many disabled people demonstrate in the course of daily living are exactly the qualities needed in all adoptive parents and foster carers (Cousins, 2006).

But oppressive values persist – perhaps most perniciously at the informal level where decision-making is less transparent. Workers and panels need to be helped to confront these prejudices which ultimately deny some children a permanent family.

For black disabled people, the discrimination is doubled (Wates, 2002); and where those applicants are single, black and minority ethnic women, the barriers at both the approval and matching stage can seem insurmountable.

We would always argue that adoption is primarily a service for children, not adults. But children would be better served if approved adults seeking a match were always supported by social workers advocating proactively alongside them. This may mean recruiting more black and disabled staff.

At the matching stage, the more variables, the more complex becomes the matching; "race" and "disability" can end up competing for priority. If a prime aim is to enhance the identity of displaced children, should we favour a black adopter or a disabled adopter for a black disabled child? Or is the disability status of the adult not relevant? There are no rules of thumb, and each child's hierarchy of needs must be thoroughly and individually assessed. We do know that black disabled children are more likely than black not-disabled children to be placed with a white family (Simon, 2000) – but in this research, the white families' disability status is unknown. Research is also lacking about the reverse perspective: to what extent, and with what outcomes, do white and black and minority ethnic disabled adults adopt white and black and minority ethnic disabled children? This would be useful in informing new thinking about recruitment processes and the development of services for these children.

At the post-adoption stage, the efficiency and effectiveness of support services will be crucial in sustaining the placement. This may be particularly so for disabled black adopters who are accessing white bureaucracies.

Recruiting black and minority ethnic adopters
Examples of good practice

Below, we offer examples of good practice which have been set up by local authorities and voluntary agencies. These are by no means exhaustive, and we are sure that other such examples exist. However, the procedures followed in the examples below could be useful and appropriate for your agency and the communities that your agency serves.

BAAF/ALG (Association of London Government) Black and Minority Ethnic Carer Recruitment Project

This project was set up in September 2002 and has funding from the ALG until March 2007. Its aim is to actively support family placement professionals with local authorities and voluntary agencies in London's 33 boroughs to achieve improved levels of recruitment of black and minority ethnic adopters and foster carers. Its support group for London-based black adopters has been meeting regularly since May 2005, providing a safe environment for examining issues and providing mutual support and learning. Its web pages on the BAAF website provide downloadable introductory guides to adopting and fostering a child in English, Hindi, Urdu, Bengali and Gujurati. This Good Practice Guide is based on the work done and lessons learned during the project.

Barnardo's Jigsaw Project

Barnardo's Jigsaw Project has been extremely successful in recruiting families with mixed heritages. Applicants must live within a 50-mile radius of its offices in Walthamstow, East London. The success of the agency's work is based upon its ethnically diverse staff group.

Families have commented on the promptness with which the agency responds to their initial call, the service they receive from the agency and the fact that they are met "half-way" by the staff and treated with respect by those who are conducting the assessment.

The agency does very little in the way of publicity. It has a regular advertisement in the Yellow Pages and a banner advertisement outside their offices. It recruits mainly by word of mouth, a method that has taken time to build up. It also publishes a newsletter.

London Borough of Southwark

The borough has a policy that information packs are sent out within 48 hours when an enquiry is made. They then follow up with a telephone call, seven days later. The borough then offers a home visit to anyone living not more than one-and-a-half hour's travel time from their offices.

PACT (Parents and Children Together)

PACT has a specific strategy for recruiting families from African-Caribbean, Asian and mixed-heritage backgrounds. One of the objectives for the project is 'to provide a culturally and linguistically sensitive service when working with children and families'. This is done by recruiting staff from a black or minority ethnic background to take a leading role in recruitment activities within the community.

NCH Black Families

The NCH Black Families project in London has been successful in recruiting black families since 2004. Their reputation is helping to build on that success. Applicants say that they have felt welcomed and valued by the agency staff. NCH Black Families responds very quickly to enquiries – within a week in most cases.

When asked about why they have approached NCH Black Families as opposed to a local authority, the resounding feedback from applicants has been that the service offered by NCH is specifically for black families. Many prospective applicants have said that when they had approached other organisations, those organisations were fronted by white management and staff and they felt that they were being judged. There was also a view that social workers' eurocentric beliefs and assumptions can get in the way and families have felt that they had to explain their culture before being assessed for their parenting skills and abilities. When they approached NCH, on the other hand, they have known from the first moment that the staff and panel members were from similar backgrounds as themselves and therefore they have not felt themselves to be judged in the same manner.

London Borough of Tower Hamlets

The London Borough of Tower Hamlets has one of the most diverse populations in the UK. With an established Bengali, white UK, Somali and African-Caribbean population and a growing Vietnamese community, their fostering and adoption teams are faced with many challenges in recruiting quality carers for looked after children.

The council has employed various strategies in order to increase the number of carers from these ethnic groups. The service has a Bangladeshi Resource Officer and a Vietnamese Community Officer who have been employed to establish links and build awareness of fostering and adoption within their communities. Additionally, there is a specialist disability worker, who focuses on the recruitment of carers for disabled children.

The department organises events in local community centres as well as London-wide conferences and festivals. Links have been created with mosques and imams to raise the profile of adoption and fostering and to promote partnership working between the community and the local authority. The recruitment materials have taken into account faith groups and have chosen to use graphic designs based on religious symbols rather than real photographs, so that posters can be displayed in places of worship and community organisations.

Recruitment campaigns use a range of media including Sunrise, Kismet and Choice FM radio stations, newspaper editorials, leaflets and outdoor media; there is extensive advertising on a Bengali digital channel called Channel S.

A member of staff says, 'Our service aims to be efficient and effective in order to reduce the number of applicants who withdraw because of the length of the assessment process. We undertake an annual survey of applicants who do not become approved foster carers to ask them their views about the service.'

Namita Singh, Adoption Team Manager, adds: "I feel that it's not just in recruitment where ethnicity matters – it's when the team reflects the kind of people we want. That engages people in a different way. Among the social worker team of 10 we have four Asians, one Caribbean, one African and four white social workers. The best way of recruiting adopters is by word of mouth and if people feel welcomed and given a fair deal, that really helps.

'We include on our website the profiles of children whom we have permission to advertise. When we home in on a family, we also show them a video of the child. All our recruitment leaflets are available in Bengali and English but I think we may need to have our assessment material translated as well.'

Manchester City Council

Manchester City Council has formed a recruitment strategy group and has appointed a worker to recruit black and minority ethnic carers. They have identified possible geographical locations to recruit from and engaged the community by making contact with faith and special interest groups. They run preparation courses related to ethnicity, such as a Somali group. They encourage carer participation in building recruitment material and the council has produced a recruitment video highlighting the need for black and minority ethnic carers.

St Francis' Children's Society–Anancy Black Families Initiative, Milton Keynes

All members of the team are of black or mixed heritage. The agency in Milton Keynes employs three community co-ordinators who undertake outreach development work to make contact with people of black and dual mixed heritage. The prospective adopters' assessments are done by the senior practitioner, who is black. The project affirms black adopters as valuable resources and promotes the strengths of black families. The key to their success is relationship-building.

The first appointment or contact is seen as crucial. Allowing people to talk about their experiences without interruptions is seen as an essential part of the process. At each stage of the assessment, there is a review of the last session, just to see if there are any problems that could be dealt with sooner rather than later. The element of intrusiveness is explained thoroughly at the very beginning of the process with openness and clarity. The whole process aims to be supportive. The management team at St Francis values its black workers and is committed to perseverance rather than quick results.

Each month a meeting is held with co-ordinators, the senior practitioner and the service manager to discuss their achievements and which areas are to be targeted next. An existing adopter is invited to these meetings to offer advice to the professionals.

The Anancy Project has also developed a leaflet that gives guidance to their social workers on assessing cultural competence.

The Khandan Initiative – now Rainbow Families

The Khandan Initiative, part of Barnardo's Scotland family placement service, was developed as a way of trying to meet the needs of Asian children requiring foster families or family-based respite care. It was successful in recruiting foster families, and won a Community Care award in 2001. The service was relaunched in 2003 by Barnardo's Scotland as Rainbow Families, which now works to develop the service to be inclusive of all black and minority ethnic children and families.

10 Conclusion

Many agencies would like to recruit more black and minority ethnic adopters to meet the needs of the children who are waiting. This is more difficult in some areas than others and there are particular challenges in reaching people from black and minority ethnic communities. There are also barriers which stand in the way. Agencies owe it to the children to break down these barriers and find adoptive parents who can offer them love and security in a new, permanent family. We hope some of the ideas and suggestions offered in this guide will help them to do that.

An influence on my culture is having been brought up in this family...It's very important for me to know my own culture. I'm always asking what's going on now, if they're having a ceremony. (Vijay, young Indian person quoted in Barn *et al*, 2005)

I have always had children around – nieces, nephews, godchildren, friends' children – but they all grew up, so the need to have children in my own life didn't strike me until I was in my mid-thirties. By then it was too late to have my own because I had developed endometriosis some time before. I ruled out the idea of artificial insemination. I couldn't afford it and also I didn't like the technology. A combination of all these factors made adoption a viable option. By the time I was 36 I had come round to it as a real possibility...

I think that people should go for it. There are a lot of children out there who would be so much better off with a home, with a family, even if there is only one of you. Black people are used to looking after extended family. Bonding simply comes from just interacting together, doing things, wiping bottoms. Children respond to affection, to being in a caring situation. I say 'Go ahead.' It might not be as easy as my situation, but it is certainly worth it. (Christine, single adopter quoted in Massiah, 2005)

References

Banks N (1995) 'Children of black mixed parentage and their placement needs', *Adoption & Fostering*, 19:2, pp19–24

Banks N (2002) 'What is a positive black identity?', in Dwivedi KN (ed) *Meeting the Needs of Ethnic Minority Children Including Refugee, Black and Mixed Parentage Children: A handbook for professionals*, London: Jessica Kingsley

Barn R, Sinclair R and Ferdinand D (1997) *Acting on Principle*, London: BAAF

Barn R, Andrew L and Mantovani N (2005) *Life After Care: The experiences of young people from different ethnic groups*, York: Joseph Rowntree Foundation

Benedictus L (21 January 2005) *The Guardian* Available at www.guardian.co.uk/britain/article/ 0,,1395534,00.html

Blueprint project, VCC (2004) *The Care Experience, Through Black Eyes* Available at www.vcc-uk.org

Braithwaite R (1962) *Paid Servant*, London: New English Library

Cabinet Office: Performance and Innovation Unit (2001) *Improving Labour Market Achievements for Ethnic Minorities in British Society: Scoping note* Available at www.strategy.gov.uk/downloads/files/ Scoping.pdf

Commission for Racial Equality (2005) *Research: Labour market statistics* Available at www.cre.gov.uk/research/statistics_ labour.html

Cousins J (2006) *Every Child is Special: Placing disabled children for permanence*, London: BAAF

Department for Education and Skills (2004) *Care Planning and Special Guardianship*, London: The Stationery Office

Department for Education and Skills (2006) *Statistics of Education: Children looked after by local authorities year ending 31 March 2005: Volume 1: National Tables*, London: The Stationery Office Available at www.dfes.gov.uk/rsgateway/DB/VOL/ v000646/vweb01-2006.pdf

Department of Health (1998) DoH circular LAC (98)20, *Adoption: Achieving the right balance*, London: Department of Health

Department of Health (2000a) *Adoption: A new approach* (White Paper), London: The Stationery Office

Department of Health (2000b) *Adoption: Regulations National Minimum Standards*, London: The Stationery Office

Department of Health (2003) *National Minimum Standards for Voluntary Adoption Agencies and Local Authority Adoption Services in England and Wales*, London: The Stationery Office

Economic & Social Research (29 March 2006) *Council Facts and Figures report* Available at www.esrcsocietytoday.ac.uk/ ESRCInfoCentre/facts/

Fahlberg V (1994) *A Child's Journey through Placement*, London, BAAF

Farmer E, Moyers S and Lees P (2004) *Children Placed with Relatives and Friends: Placement patterns and outcomes*, Bristol: University of Bristol Centre for Family Policy and Child Welfare Available at www.bris.ac.uk/sps/research/fpcw/ completed.shtml

Fostering Network (2004) *Survey: The shortage of foster carers* Available at www.fostering.net/carers/shortage.php

Fostering Network (2005) *Improving Effectiveness in Foster Care Recruitment*, London: Fostering Network

Frazer L and Selwyn J (2005) 'Why are we waiting? The demography of adoption for children of black, Asian and black mixed parentage in England', *Child and Family Social Work*, 10, pp135–147

General Register Office for Scotland (2003) *Census 2001*, Edinburgh: General Register Office for Scotland

Gill O and Jackson B (1983) *Adoption and Race*, London: Batsford Academic and Education Ltd/St Martins Press Inc

Greater London Authority (2004) *The State of London's Children Report*, London: Greater London Authority

Harris P (ed) (2006) *In Search of Belonging: Reflections by transracially adopted people*, London: BAAF

Home Office (1999) *The Stephen Lawrence Inquiry: Report of an inquiry by Sir William Macpherson of Cluny*, London: The Stationery Office

Home Office Advisory Council on Child Care (1970) *Guide to Adoption Practice*, London: Home Office

Ivaldi G (2000) *Surveying Adoption: A comprehensive analysis of local authority adoptions 1998–1998 (England)*, London: BAAF

Kirton D (2000) *"Race", Ethnicity and Adoption*, Buckingham: Open University Press

Massiah H (2005) *Looking after our Own: The stories of black and Asian adopters*, London: BAAF

MORI (2001) Poll on attitudes to adoption Available at www.baaf.org.uk/info/lpp/law/adbillbrief05_02.pdf

Office for National Statistics (2002) *Social Focus in Brief: Ethnicity 2002*, London: The Stationery Office Available at www.statistics.gov.uk/downloads/theme_social/social_focus_in_brief/ethnicity/ethnicity.pdf

Office for National Statistics (2002) *Census 2001*, London: The Stationery Office

Office of the United Nations High Commissioner for Human Rights (1989) *Convention on the Rights of the Child*, Geneva, Switzerland: Office of the United Nations High Commissioner for Human Rights

Performance and Innovation Unit (2001) *Ethnic Minorities Economic Performance: Surveying literature to emphasis facts, analysis, and likely patterns for the future*, London: Cabinet Office

Phillips M (2000) *Thematic Analysis Of Quality Protects Maps: Black and minority ethnic children and their families*, Draft 3 Available at www.dfes.gov.uk/qualityprotects/docs/ethnic.doc

Prevatt-Goldstein B (2000) 'Ethnicity and placement: beginning the debate. An interview with John Small', *Adoption & Fostering*, 24:1, pp9–14

Prevatt-Goldstein B and Spencer M (2000) *"Race" and Ethnicity: A consideration of issues for black, minority ethnic and white children in family placement*, London: BAAF

Rowe J and Lambert L (1973) *Children who Wait*, London: BAAF

Rushton A (2003) *The Adoption of Looked After Children: A scoping review of research*, London: SCIE

Scottish Executive (2002, revised 2005) *National Care Standards: adoption agencies*, Edinburgh, Scottish Executive

Scottish Executive (2002, revised 2005) *National Care Standards: foster care and family placement service*, Edinburgh, Scottish Executive

Scottish Office (1997) *Scotland's Children: The Children (Scotland) Act 1995, Regulations and Guidance* – Volume 2: *Children Looked After by Local Authorities*; Volume 3: *Adoption and Parental Responsibilities Orders*, Edinburgh: HMSO Available at www.scotland.gov.uk under Publications, Care and Social Work, 12 October 2004

Selwyn J, Frazer L and Fitzgerald A (2004) *Finding Adoptive Families for Black, Asian and Black Mixed-Parentage Children: Agency policy and practice*, London: National Children's Home

Simon J (2000) 'Disabled children in long-term fostering and adoption', *Adoption & Fostering*, 24:4, pp57–59

Singh S (2002) 'Assessing Asian families in Scotland: a discussion', in Hill M (ed) *Shaping Childcare Practice in Scotland: Key papers on adoption and fostering*, London: BAAF

Singh S, Macfadyen S and Gillies A (2002) 'To attach and belong', in Sashdev D and Meeuwen A (eds) *Are we Listening yet?*, London: Barnardo's

Small J (1986) 'Transracial placements: conflicts and contradictions', in Ahmed S, Cheetham J and Small J (eds) *Social Work with Black Children and their Families*, London: BT Batsford

Social Services Inspectorate, Department of Health (2000) *CI (2000) 7 on LAC (98) 20 – Adoption: Achieving the Right Balance: Response to Issues arising from SSI survey of local authority social service departments' implementation of the circular*, London: The Stationery Office

Sunmonu Y (2000) 'Work in progress: why black carers are deterred from adoption', *Adoption & Fostering*, 24:1, pp59–60

Thoburn J, Norford L and Rashid S (1998) *Permanent Family Placement for Children of Minority Ethnic Origin*, London: Department of Health

Thoburn J (1994) *Child Placement: Principles and Practice*, Aldershot: Ashgate

Thoburn J, Chand A and Procter J (2005) *Child Welfare Services for Minority Ethnic Families*, London: Jessica Kingsley

Triseliotis J, Feast J and Kyle F (2005) *The Adoption Triangle Revisited: A study of adoption, search and reunion experiences*, London: BAAF

Wates M (2002) 'Disability and adoption: how unexamined attitudes discriminate against disabled people as parents', *Adoption & Fostering*, 26:2, pp49–56

White A (December 2002) *Social Focus in Brief: Ethnicity 2002*, London: Office for National Statistics

Appendix 1: Useful reading

Ahmed S (2004) *Preventative Services for Black and Minority Ethnic Children and Families: A review of recent literature*, The National Evaluation of the Children's Fund
Available at www.ne-cf.org

Argent H (ed) (2003) *Models of Adoption Support: What works and what doesn't*, London: BAAF

Arnold E (1997) *Out of Sight – Not out of Mind: Studies in inter-cultural social work*, Birmingham: British Association of Social Workers

Barn R (ed) (1999) *Working with Black Children and Adolescents in Need*, London: BAAF

Dwivedi KN (2002) *Meeting the Needs of Ethnic Minority Children, including Refugee, Black and Mixed Parentage Children: A handbook for professionals*, London: Jessica Kingsley

Fenton R (2001) 'Initial agency responses to black prospective adopters: results of a small-scale study', *Adoption & Fostering*, 25:1, pp13–23

Flynn R (2000) 'Black carers for white children: shifting the "same-race" placement debate', *Adoption & Fostering*, 24:1, pp47–52

Fostering Network (2004) *Good Practice Guidelines for the Recruitment of Foster Carers*, London: Fostering Network

Harris P (ed) (2006) *In Search of Belonging: Reflections by transracially adopted people*, London: BAAF

Ince L (1998) *Making it Alone: A study of the care experiences of young black people*, London: BAAF

Joseph Rowntree Foundation (2004) 'Experiencing ethnicity: Discrimination and service provision', York: Joseph Rowntree Foundation

Kidane S (2001) *'I did not choose to come here': Listening to refugee children*, London: BAAF

Kirton D, Feast J and Howe D (2000) 'Searching, reunion and transracial adoption', *Adoption & Fostering*, 24:3, pp6–18

Luckock B and Hart A (2005) 'Adoptive family life and adoption support: policy ambivalence and the development of effective services', *Child & Family Social Work*, 10:2, pp125–134

Madge N (2001) *Understanding Difference: The meaning of ethnicity for young lives*, London: National Children's Bureau

O'Hagan K (2001) *Cultural Competence in the Caring Professions*, London: Jessica Kingsley

Parekh B (2000) *The Future of Multi-Ethnic Britain: Report of the commission on the future of multi-ethnic Britain: The Parekh Report, Runnymemde Trust*, London: Profile Books

Pierson J (2002) *Tackling Social Exclusion*, Routledge: London

Rashid, SP (2000) 'The strengths of black families: appropriate placements for all', *Adoption & Fostering*, 24:1, pp15–22

Richards A and Ince L (2000) *Overcoming the Obstacles: Looked after children quality services for BME children and their families*, London: Family Rights Group

Sachdev D and Meeuwen AV (2002) *Are we Listening yet? Working with minority ethnic communities: some models of practice*, Ilford: Barnardo's

Small J with Prevatt-Goldstein B (ed) (2000) 'Ethnicity in placement: beginning the debate', *Adoption & Fostering*, 24:1, pp9–14

Thoburn J, Norford L and Rashid S (2000) *Permanent Family Placement for Children of Minority Ethnic Origin*, London: Jessica Kingsley

Tizard B (1991) 'Intercountry adoption, a review of the evidence', *Journal of Child Psychology & Psychiatry*, 22:5, pp 743–756

Wignall P (2002) *Multicultural Britain*, Oxford: Heinemann Library

Appendix 2: Minority ethnic media

Newspapers, periodicals and websites

The following details of newspapers, periodicals and websites are intended merely as a starting point for either advertising possibilities or for making contact with certain communities. This is not a comprehensive list but hopefully it will help you to explore alternative routes when targeting certain communities.

Arabic

Al Arab
159 Acre Lane, London SW2 5UA
Tel: 020 7021 0966
Fax: 020 7021 0917
Email: edit@alarab.co.uk
www.alarab.co.uk
Format: Newspaper
Language: Arabic
Frequency: Daily

Al Hayat
Kensington Centre, 66 Hammersmith Road
London W14 8YT
Tel: 020 7602 9988
Fax: 020 7602 4963
Email: robert@alhayat.com
www.alhayat.com
Format: Newspaper
Language: Arabic
Frequency: Daily

"Asharq Al Awsat"
182–184 High Holborn, London WC1V 7AP
Tel: 020 7404 6950
Fax: 020 7404 6963
Email: moira@alkaleejiah.co.uk
www.asharqalawsat.com
Format: Newspaper
Language: Arabic
Frequency: Daily/Weekly
Other publications: Almajalla, Sayidaty, Hia, Aljamila, Alrajoul

Al-Ahram International
Al-Ahram House, 203–209 North Gower Street,
London NW1 2NJ
Tel: 020 7388 1155
Fax: 020 7388 3130

Format: Newspaper
Language: Arabic
Frequency: Daily

Al-Muntada
The Iraqi Community Association
Pallingswick House, 241 King Street, London W6 9LP
Tel: 020 8741 5491
Fax: 020 8748 9010
Email: iraqicommunity@btclick.com
www.iraqicommunity.org
Format: Newspaper
Language: Arabic/English
Frequency: Quarterly

HIA
Arab Press House, 182–184 High Holborn
London WC1V 7AP
Tel: 020 7831 8181
Fax: 020 7831 2310
Email: editorial@asharqalawsat.com
www.asharqalawsat.com
Format: Magazine
Language: Arabic
Frequency: Monthly

The Middle East

IC Publications
7 Coldbath Square, London EC1R 4LQ
Tel: 020 7713 7711
Fax: 020 7713 7898
Email: icpubs@africiasia.com
www.africasia.com
Format: Magazine
Language: English
Frequency: Monthly

Persian Channel (The)
PO Box 2821, London NW2 1ES
Tel: 020 8731 9333
Format: TV
Language: Farsi

Asian

ARY Digital (TV)
65 North Acton Road, Park Royal, London NW10 6PJ
Tel: 020 8838 6300
Fax: 020 8838 6122
Email: arydigital@ukonline.co.uk
www.arydigital.tv
Format: Satellite
Language: English, Urdu, Hindi

Asians in Media
www.asiansinmedia.com
This website is aimed at the Asian community and has articles related to different media. It is a good site for posting up-and-coming events.

Asian Image
Newsquest Media Group, Newspaper House
1 High Street, Blackburn, Lancashire BB1 1HT
Tel: 01254 298 263
Email: skhan@lancashire.newsquest.co

Asian Leader
48 Milkstone Road, Rochdale, Lancashire OL11 1EB
Tel: 01706 355045
Fax: 01706 649908
Email: sales@asianleader.co.uk
www.asianleader.co.uk
Format: Newspaper
Language: All Asian groups
Frequency: Fortnightly

Asian News
Observer Buildings, Drake Street, Rochdale OL15 1PH
Tel: 01706 357086
Fax: 01706 341595
Email: asiannews@gmwn.co.uk
www.asiannews.co.uk
Format: Newspaper
Language: English
Frequency: Monthly

Asian Sound Radio
Globe House, Southall Street, Manchester M3 1LG
Tel: 0161 288 1000
Fax: 0161 288 9000
Email: news@asiansoundradio.fsbusiness.co.uk
www.asiansoundradio.co.uk
Format: Radio
Language: English, Urdu, Bengali, Gujarati, Punjabi
Frequency: Daily

Asian Times
Unit 2.01, Whitechapel Technology Centre
65 Whitechapel Road, London E1 1DU
Tel: 020 7650 2000
Fax: 020 7650 2001
Email: asiantimes@ethnicmedia.co.uk
www.ethnicmedia.co.uk
Format: Newspaper
Language: English
Frequency: Weekly national publication

Asian Trader
Garavi Gijarat House, 1 Silex Street
London SE1 0DW
Tel: 020 7928 1234
Fax: 020 7261 0055
Email: shailesh@gujarat.co.uk
www.gg2.net
Format: Magazine
Language: English
Frequency: Weekly

Asian Voice
Karama Yoga House, 12 Hoxton Market
London N1 6HW
Tel: 020 7749 4080
Fax: 020 7739 0358
Email: aveditorial@abplgroup.com
www.abplgroup.com
Format: Newspaper
Language: English/Gujarati
Frequency: Weekly

Awaaz Asian Voice
PO Box 15, Batley, West Yorkshire WF17 7YY
Tel: 01924 510512
Fax: 01924 510513
Email: shkir@awaaznews.com
www.awaaznews.co.uk
Format: Newspaper
Language: English, Urdu, Gujarati
Frequency: Monthly

Awaze Quam International
Gate 2, Unit 5b, Booth Street, Smethwick
Birmingham B66 2PF
Tel: 0121 555 5921
Fax: 0121 555 6899
Email: awazequam@yahoo.co.uk
Format: Newspaper
Language: Bi-lingual English and Punjabi
Frequency: Weekly

Barfi Culture
www.barficulture.com
Barfi Culture is an online magazine and community website primarily populated by the British Asian community – India, Pakistan, Bangladesh and Sri Lanka.

Clickwalla
www.clickwalla.com
This website bridges the gap between mainstream organisations, Asian businesses and the Asian community in the UK.

Daily Jang (The)
Jang Publications Ltd, 1 Sanctuary Street
London SE1 1ED
Tel: 020 7403 5833
Fax: 020 7378 1653
Email: editor@janglondon.co.uk
www.jang.com.pk
Format: Newspaper
Language: Urdu/English
Frequency: Daily

Eastern Eye
Unit 2.01, Whitechapel Technology Centre
65 Whitechapel Road, London E1 1DU
Tel: 020 7650 2000
Fax: 020 7650 2001
Email: newsdesk@easterneyeuk.co.uk
www.ethnicmedia.co.uk
Format: Newspaper
Language: English
Frequency: Weekly

Garavi Gujarat
Garavi Gujarat House, 1–2 Silex Street
London SE1 0DW
Tel: 020 7928 1234
Fax: 020 7261 0055
Email: garavi@gujarat.co.uk
www.gg2.net
Format: Newspaper
Language: Gujarati/English
Frequency: Weekly

Gujarat Samachar
Karma Yoga House, Unit 2, 12 Hoxton Market
London N1 6HG
Tel: 020 7749 4098
Email: urja@abplgroup.com
www.abplgroup.com

Format: Newspaper
Language: Gujarati/English
Frequency: Weekly

Impact International
Suite B, PO Box 2493, 233 Seven Sisters Road
London N4 2BL
Tel: 020 7263 1417
Fax: 020 7272 8934
Email: infor@impact-magazine.com
Format: Magazine
Language: Aimed at Muslim communities
Frequency: Monthly

India Link International
42 Farm Avenue, North Harrow, Middlesex HA2 7LR
Tel: 020 8866 8421
Fax: 020 8248 8417
Email: indialink@hotmail.com
www.indialink-online.com
Format: Magazine
Language: English
Frequency: Bi-monthly

India Monitor
FPA, 11 Carlton House Terrace, London SW1Y 5AJ
Tel: 020 8325 6358
Email: sawaal@aol.com
www.indiamonitor.com
Format: Web magazine
Language: English
Frequency: Weekly

Janomot
Unit 2, 20B Spelman Street, London E1 5LQ
Tel: 020 7377 6032
Fax: 020 7247 0141
Email: jsnomot@easynet.co.uk
Format: Newspaper
Language: Bengali
Frequency: Weekly

Milap Weekly
Masbro Centre, 87 Masbro Road, London W14 0LR
Tel: 020 7385 8966
Fax: 020 7385 8966
Format: Newspaper
Language: Urdu
Frequency: Weekly

Muslim Directory
65a Grosvenor Road, London W7 1HR
Tel: 020 8799 4455
Fax: 020 8799 4456
Email: info@muslimdirectory.co.uk
Format: Directory
Language: English
Frequency: Annual

Muslim News (The)
PO Box 380, Harrow, Middlesex HA2 6LL
Tel: 020 8863 8586
Fax: 020 8863 9370
Email: info@muslimnews.co.uk
www.muslimnews.co.uk
Format: Newspaper
Language: English
Frequency: Monthly

Nation (The)
Links Media, 96b Ilford Lane, Ilford, Essex IG1 2LD
Tel: 020 8478 3200
Fax: 020 8478 6200
Email: msarwar@thenation.co.uk
www.thenation.co.uk
Format: Newspaper
Language: English/Urdu
Frequency: Daily

Navin Weekly
Masbro Centre, 87 Masbro Road, London W14 0LR
Tel: 020 7385 8966
Fax: 020 7385 8966
Format: Newspaper
Language: Hindi
Frequency: Weekly

News (The)
Jang Publications Ltd, 1 Sanctuary Street
London SE1 1ED
Tel: 020 7403 5833
Fax: 020 7378 1653
Email: editor@janglondon.co.uk
www.jang.com
Format: Newspaper
Language: English/Urdu
Frequency: Daily

New Horizon
12–14 Barkat House, 116–118 Finchley Road
London NW3 5HT
Tel: 020 7245 0404
Fax: 020 7245 9769
Email: iibi@islamic-banking.com
www.islamic-banking.com

Format: Magazine
Language: English
Frequency: Monthly

New World
234 Holloway Road, London N7 8DA
Tel: 020 7700 2673
Format: Magazine
Language: English
Frequency: Weekly

Notun Din
46g Greatorex Street, London E1 5NP
Tel: 020 747 6280
Fax: 020 7247 9993
Format: Newspaper
Language: Bengali
Frequency: Weekly

Punjabi Guardian (The)
129 Soho Road, Handsworth, Birmingham B21 9ST
Tel: 0121 554 3995
Fax: 0121 507 1065
Format: Newspaper
Language: Punjabi/English
Frequency: Monthly

Punjab Mail International
66 Dames Road, Forest Gate, London E7 0DR
Tel: 020 8522 0901
Fax: 020 8522 0901
Format: Magazine
Language: Punjabi/English
Frequency: Monthly

Punjab Times International
24 Cotton Brook Road
Sir Francis Ley Industrial Park, Derby DE23 8YJ
Tel: 01332 372851
Fax: 01332 372833
Email: punjabtimes@aol.com
Format: Newspaper
Language: Punjabi/English
Frequency: Weekly

Q News International Ltd
PO Box 4295, London W1A 7YH
Tel: 07985 176 798
Email: info@q-news.com
Website: www.q-news.com
Format: Magazine
Language: English
Frequency: Monthly

Radio XL
KMS House, Bradford Street, Birmingham B12 0JD
Tel: 0121 753 5353
Fax: 0121 753 3111
Email: arun@radioxl.net
Website: www.radioxl.net
Format: Radio
Language: English, Hindi, Urdu, Punjabi,
Bengali, Gujarati, Mirpuri
Frequency: Daily

Red Hot Curry
Unit 28, I/O Centre, Hearle Way, Hatfield
Business Park, Hatfield AL10 9EW
Tel: 01707 269666
Fax: 01707 269676
www.redhotcurry.com
Format: Web magazine
Language: English
Frequency: Daily

Sabras Sound
Radio House, 63 Melton Road, Leicester LE4 6PN
Tel: 0116 261 0666
Fax: 0116 268 7776
Email: sales@sabrasradio.com
www.sabrasradio.com
Format: Radio
Language: English, Hindi, Gujurati, Bengali, Punjabi
Frequency: Daily

Sikh Courier International (The)
33 Wargrave Road, South Harrow
Middlesex HA2 8LL
Tel: 020 8864 9228
Format: Magazine
Language: English
Frequency: Quarterly

Sikh Messenger (The)
43 Dorset Road, Merton Park, London SW19 3EZ
Tel: 020 8540 4148
Email: sikhmessenger@aol.com
www.nsouk.co.uk
Format: Magazine
Language: English
Frequency: Quarterly

Sony Entertainment TV Asia
34 Fouberts Place, London W1F 7PX
Tel: 020 7534 7575
Fax: 020 7534 7585
www.asiaset.tv

Format: Television
Language: Hindi
Frequency: Daily

Sunrise Radio Ltd
Sunrise House, Sunrise Road, Southall
Middlesex UB2 4AU
Tel: 020 8574 6666
Fax: 020 8813 8900
Email: reception@sunriseradio.com
www.sunriseradio.com
Format: Radio
Language: Asian
Frequency: Daily

Weekly Des Pardes
8 The Crescent, Southall, Middlesex UB1 1BE
Tel: 020 8571 1127
Fax: 020 8571 2604
Format: Newspaper
Language: Punjabi
Frequency: Weekly

Weekly Potrika
218 Jubilee Street, London E1 3BS
Tel: 020 7423 9270
Fax: 020 7423 9122
Format: Newspaper
Language: Bengali
Frequency: Weekly

Zee Network (TV)
Belvue Business Centre, Belvue Road, Northolt,
Middlesex UB5 5QQ
Tel: 020 8839 4035
Fax: 020 8841 3319
www.zeetv.co.uk
Format: Television
Language: English and all South Asian languages
Frequency: Daily

Black

African Business
IC Publications, 7 Coldbath Square, London EC1 4LQ
Tel: 020 7713 7711
Fax: 020 7713 7898
Email: icpubs@africasia.com
www.africasia.com/africanbusiness/
Format: Magazine
Language: English
Frequency: Monthly

African Voice
Afro Hollywood, Unit 7 Holles House, Overton Road
London SW9 7JN
Tel: 020 7274 3933
Fax: 020 7274 4873
Format: Newspaper
Language: English
Frequency: Weekly

Black Britain Online
Suite 5, Culvert House, Culvert Road
London SW11 5AP
Tel: 020 7498 5656
Fax: 020 7498 5757
Email: info@blackbritain.co.uk
www.blackbritain.co.uk
Format: Web pages
Language: English
Frequency: Daily
This online portal is for community news, information, e-commerce and serves as the central point of web entry to the Colourful Network.

Black Film Maker
Suite 13, 5 Blackhorse Lane, London E17 6DS
Tel: 020 8531 9111
Email: bfm@bfmmedia.com
www.bfmmedia.com
Format: Magazine
Language: English
Frequency: Bi-monthly

Black Beauty and Hair Magazine
Hawker Consumer Publications, Culvert House
Culvert Road, London SW11 5DH
Tel: 020 7720 2108
www.blackbeautyandhair.com
Format: Magazine
Language: English
Frequency: Bi-monthly

Black Information Link (BLINK)
Suite 12, Winchester House, 9 Cranmer Road
London SW9 6EJ
Tel: 020 7582 1990
Fax: 020 7793 8269
Email: blink1990@blink.org.uk
www.blink.org.uk
This internet portal is run by the 1990 Trust, a black organisation, and includes sections on everything from art and culture to the Stephen Lawrence campaign and the environment.

Black Net UK
46 Deptford Broadway, London SE8 4PH
Tel: 0870 746 500/020 8692 9755
www.blacknet.co.uk
This website is for black people from around the world to come together to share experiences and ideas. Blacknet UK is also encouraging communities to rise above racism and promote cultural respect within society with a view to reduce cultural conflict and misunderstandings.

Black UK Online
PO Box 574, Bury St Edmunds, Suffolk IP31 3WZ
www.blackukonline.com
This website provides a blend of local, national and international news, lifestyle, views, reviews, profiles and entertainment. The aim of the site is to 'widen thought provoking editorial beyond the black experience and to reflect more fully the multicultural Britain that we live in today'.

Black Variety TV
7 Raleigh Grove, Luton LU4 8RE
Tel: 01582 581753
Email: info@bvtv.co.uk
www.bvtv.co.uk
Format: Satellite television
Language: English
Frequency: Daily

Caribbean Times
Unit 2.01, Whitechapel Technology Centre
65 Whitechapel Road, London E1 1DU
Tel: 020 7650 2000
Fax: 020 7650 2001
Email: caribbeantimes@ethnicmedia.co.uk
www.ethnicmedia.co.uk
Format: Newspaper
Language: English
Frequency: Weekly

Choice FM
PO Box 969, London WC2H 7BB
Tel: 020 7766 6000
Fax: 020 7766 6100
Email: ivor.etienne@choicefm.com
www.choicefm.net
Format: Radio
Language: English
Frequency: Daily

Galaxy 105
Joseph's Well, Hanover Walk, Leeds LS3 1AB
Tel: 0113 213 1053
Fax: 0113 213 1054
Email: news105@galaxy105.co.uk
www.galaxy105.co.uk
Format: Radio
Language: English
Frequency: Daily

Kiss 100 FM
Mappin House, 4 Winsley Street, London W1W 8HF
Tel: 020 7975 8100
www.kiss100.com
Format: Radio
Language: English
Frequency: Daily

Mauritius News
583 Wandsworth Road, London SW8 3JD
Tel: 020 7498 3066
Fax: 020 76279 0939
Email: editor@mauritiusnews.co.uk
www.mauritiusnews.co.uk
Format: Newspaper
Language: English
Frequency: Monthly

New African
IC Publications, 7 Coldbath Square, London EC1R 4LQ
Tel: 020 7713 7711
Fax: 020 7713 7898
Email: icpubs@africasia.com
www.africasia.com/newafrican/
Format: Magazine
Language: English
Frequency: Monthly

New Nation
Unit 2, Whitechapel Technology Centre
65 Whitechapel Road, London E1 1DU
Tel: 020 760 2000
Email: michelle@newnation.co.uk
www.newnation.co.uk
Format: Newspaper
Language: English
Frequency: Weekly

Pride Magazine
55 Battersea Bridge Road, London SW11 3AX
Tel: 020 7228 3110
Email: info@pridemagazine.com
www.pridemagazine.com
Format: Magazine
Language English
Frequency: Monthly

Vibin
95 Barndale Road, Liverpool L18 7MY
Tel: 0781 667 8618
Email: info@vibinmusic.co.uk
www.vibinmusic.co.uk
Format: Music website
Language: English
Frequency: Weekly

Voice (The)
The Voice Group Ltd, 8th Floor, Blue Star House
234–244 Stockwell Road, London SW9 8SP
Tel: 020 7737 7377
Fax: 020 7274 8994
www.voice-online.co.uk
Format: Newspaper
Language: English
Frequency: Weekly

Chinese

British Born Chinese
www.britishbornchinese.org.uk
This community website is run by a not-for-profit organisation staffed by volunteers. It provides a forum in which British-born Chinese people can share experiences, ideas and thoughts.

Chinatown Online
www.chinatown-online.co.uk
The website provides a guide to the Chinese in the UK and Greater China. It covers culture, travel, food and business. It is a non-political, non-religious and non-partisan site.

Chinese in Britain Forum

1st Floor, Boardman House, 64 Broadway
London E15 1NG
Tel: 020 8432 0681
Fax: 020 8432 0685
Email: info@cibf.co.uk
www.cibf.co.uk

The Chinese Channel

Teddington Studios, Broom Road, Teddington
Middlesex TW11 9NT
Tel: 020 8614 8300
Fax: 020 8943 0982
Email: tvbseurope@chinese-channel.co.uk
www.chinese-channel.co.uk
Format: Satellite television
Language: Cantonese, Mandarin
Frequency: Daily

Chinese News & Entertainment

7th Floor, Chiswick Centre, 414 Chiswick High Road
London W4 5TF
Tel: 020 8947 4320
www.phoenixcne.com
Format: Satellite television
Language: Chinese

Sing Tao Daily

46 Dean Street, London W1V 5AP
Tel: 020 8732 7628
Email: editor@singtao.co.uk
www.singtao.co.uk
Format: Newspaper
Language: Chinese
Frequency: Daily

Filipino

Filipino Observer (The)

PO Box 20376, Golders Green
London NW11 8FE
Tel: 020 8731 7195
Fax: 020 8905 5620
Email: editor@filipino-observer.com
www.filipino-observer.com
Format: Newspaper
Language: English
Frequency: Monthly

Greek

Helenic TV (TV)

50 Clarendon Road, London N8 0DJ
Tel: 020 8292 7037
Fax: 020 8292 7042
Email: helenictv.net@yahoo.co.uk
www.helenictv.net
Format: Television
Language: Greek
Frequency: Daily

Parikiaki

144 Falkland Road, London N8 0NP
Tel: 020 8341 0751
Format: Newspaper
Language: Greek
Frequency: Weekly

Irish

Irish Post

Irish Post Media UK, Cambridge House
Cambridge Grove, Hammersmith, London W6 0LE
Tel: 020 8741 0649
Fax: 020 8741 3382
Email: info@irishpost.co.uk
www.irishpost.co.uk
Format: Newspaper
Language: English
Frequency: Weekly

Irish World

934 North Circular Road, London NW2 7JR
Tel: 020 8453 7800
Fax: 020 8208 1103
Email: admin@theirishworld.com
www.theirishworld.com
Format: Newspaper
Language: English
Frequency: Weekly

Jewish

Board of Deputies of British Jews
www.bod.org.uk
This website protects, supports and defends the rights and interests, and religious rights and customs of Jews and the Jewish community in the UK.

Jewish Chronicle
25 Furnival Street, London EC4A 1JT
Tel: 020 7415 1500
Fax: 020 7831 5188
Email: alanrubinstein@thejc.com
www.thejc.com
Format: Newspaper
Language: English
Frequency: Weekly

Jewish Recorder
69 Mossfield Road, Kings Heath
Birmingham B14 7JE
Tel: 0161 740 9321
Fax: 0161 740 9325
Email: editors@recorder.org.uk
Format: Magazine
Language: English
Frequency: Monthly

Jewish Tribune
95–97 Stamford Hill, London N16 5DN
Tel: 020 8800 6688
Fax: 020 8800 5000
Email: ads@jewishtribune.com
www.jewishtribune.com
Format: Newspaper
Language: English/Yiddish
Frequency: Weekly

Turkish

Hurriyet
1st Floor, 35 D'Arblay Street, London W1V 3FE
Tel: 020 7734 1211
Fax: 020 7287 3101
Email: zaci@btconnect.com
Format: Newspaper
Language: Turkish
Frequency: Daily

London Turkish Radio
185b High Road, London N22 6BA
Tel: 020 8881 0606
Email: info@londonturkishradio.org
www.londonturkishradio.org
Format: Radio
Language: Turkish
Frequency: Daily

Toplum Postasi
117 Green Lanes, London N16 9DN
Tel: 020 7354 4424
Fax: 020 7354 0313
Email: info@toplumpostasi.net
www.toplumpostasi.net
Format: Newspaper
Language: Turkish/English
Frequency: Weekly

Multi-ethnic

Spectrum Radio
4 Ingate Place, Queenstown Road
London SW8 3NS
Tel: 020 7627 4433
Fax: 020 7627 3409
Email: enquiries@spectrumradio.net
www.spectrumradio.net
Format: Radio
Language: Various
Frequency: Daily

Intermix
www.intermix.org.uk
Intermix.org.uk is a website for mixed-race families, individuals and anyone who feels they have a multiracial identity and wants to take part.

The Inter Faith Network for the UK
5–7 Tavistock Place, London WC1H 9SN
Tel: 020 7388 0008
Fax: 020 7388 7124
This agency links over 90 faith communities, interfaith and educational bodies. The ethos is to promote good relationships and give useful advice and information.

Appendix 3: Useful organisations

Adoption and fostering

British Association for Adoption and Fostering (BAAF)
Head Office
Saffron House
6–10 Kirby Street
London
EC1N 8TS
Tel: 020 7421 2600
www.baaf.org.uk

BAAF Cymru
7 Cleeve House
Lambourne Crescent
Cardiff
CF14 5GP
Tel: 029 2076 1155

BAAF Northern Ireland
Botanic House
1–5 Botanic Avenue
Belfast
BT7 1JG
Tel: 028 9031 5494

BAAF Scotland
40 Shandwick Place
Edinburgh
EH2 4RT
Tel: 0131 2204749

Adoption UK
46 The Green
South Bar Street
Banbury
OX16 9AB
Tel: 01295 752240
www.adoptionuk.org

Fostering Network
87 Blackfriars Road
London
SE1 8HA
Tel: 020 7620 6400
www.fostering.net

Fostering Network Wales
Suite 11, 2nd Floor
Bay Chambers
West Bute Street
Cardiff
CF10 5BB
Tel: 029 2044 0940

Fostering Network Northern Ireland
Unit 10
40 Montgomery Road
Belfast
BT6 9HL
Tel: 028 9070 5056

Fostering Network Scotland
Ingram House
2nd Floor
227 Ingram Street
Glasgow G1 1DA
Tel: 0141 204 1400

Websites for and about black/minority ethnic communities

Black UK Online
www.blackukonline.com/
A website covering news, jobs, heritage, health, youth issues and other information.

Black Britain
www.blackbritain.co.uk
A website covering news, business, entertainment and jobs, with links to a digital radio station.

Red Hot Curry
www.redhotcurry.co.uk
A website aimed at the British Asian community, covering news, lifestyle, property and shopping.

www.bbc.co.uk/religion
For information about different religions, beliefs and customs.